The Journey to No-Self

The Journey to No-Self

A Personal Account of the Mystical Experience

by

Patrick Drysdale

NEW FALCON PUBLICATIONS
TEMPE, ARIZONA, U.S.A.

International Standard Book Number: 1-56184-136-6
Library of Congress Catalog Card Number: 97-81138

First Edition 1998

Cover art by Amanda Fisher

The paper used in this publication meets the minimum requirements of the American National Standard for Permanence of Paper for Printed Library Materials Z39.48-1984

Address all inquiries to:
NEW FALCON PUBLICATIONS
1739 East Broadway Road Suite 1-277
Tempe, AZ 85282 U.S.A.
(or)
320 East Charleston Blvd. • Suite 204-286
Las Vegas, NV 89104 U.S.A.

website: http://www.newfalcon.com
email: info@newfalcon.com

DEDICATED TO
SINCERE SEEKERS
OF
TRUTH

TABLE OF CONTENTS

Foreword

Keep in mind that you will read an account of an inner journey that very few ever take. Most people don't embark on this inner voyage because they don't know that such a state as inner freedom exists. If you try to tell them that union with God is possible *in this life*, they either don't believe you or think you are crazy. The voyage is not all ecstasy and bliss but the experiences of intense love and joy more than compensate for the time spent wandering in the dark.

The choice to make this inner journey was not mine. When the ship of life moved, it took me with it and I had no say or control in the matter. It's important to keep in mind that we all start from different directions, pass through different sets of events and that no two inner journeys can possibly be alike. I'm firmly convinced that the inner experiences generated by these events, though, are identical for everyone.

The person who says yes at the start to the inner journey and then calls a halt when the going becomes uncertain or frightening probably is not a true mystic to begin with because the mystic is one who says *Yes* to life's experiences, rapids and all. Spiritual courage is adventurous and likes to explore unknown territory and is not afraid to walk where angels fear to tread.

Part of this great inner adventure is to touch upon unusual dimensions of the soul and take psychological risks without preconceived notions of what the outcome will be. Since everyone knows how to get as far as the stream and since heaven can take care of itself, what we need to know is something about the crossing. The mystic needs to describe the passage as best he can. Even if very few understand what he says, he will at least let those few know that such a transition is possible *in this life* and hopefully ease their fear during the crossing over.

Mystical authors have performed a great disservice to God and humanity by writing only about their ecstatic illuminations that came in a flurry of visions and voices but surprisingly these same authors remain suspiciously silent *after the visions have stopped.* This, unfortunately, has left us with a lopsided view of the *total awakening experience.* My aim is to give a comprehensive view of the inner journey, both the highs and the lows, and I have recorded the occurrences in chronological order so that the reader can get a more balanced picture of what to expect down the road.

I've compared my journals with those of other mystical authors and found that the experiences leading to Truth are remarkably similar across the board. The outer circumstances are different for various periods but the inner experiences they generate are the *same for everyone* and are even described in similar ways by mystics in different cultures and time periods.

I discovered that there are a few accounts by Catholic saints who described both the highs and the lows of the spiritual experience but not much chronicled by modern day mystics. The annals that I found helped me realize that I was going through necessary stages and that trust in God was absolutely essential at every step. I was so grateful to those authors for leaving behind their psychological maps that I recorded my own just to say *Thank you* and hope that it may help someone else along the way.

Patrick Drysdale
Medford, OR

INTRODUCTION

The purpose of this book is to present a clear overview of the enlightenment experience from the meager beginnings of the ego to the realization of the True Self.

The mystical journey is not easy to articulate and this is probably the reason why so little has been written about it, which is of no help to people like me who take the journey and then wonder why no one else has said anything about it. Experiential literature of modern day mystics is not widely available and what I couldn't find anywhere was an understandable, spiritual, step-by-step account of the total experience of the loss of self. Such an account in mystical literature is conspicuously lacking and this is what prompted me to record my own.

Most people don't know how practical mysticism really is. A mystic is not someone who has retired from the world but is actively involved with it and lives more fearlessly than most people because he's faced all his embarrassing weaknesses and broken through false self images while others are still nervously working very hard at keeping theirs from being exposed. The mystic looks like everyone else, works in the office and stands in the 10 items or less express lane in the grocery store but he knows something others don't. He knows that God is a *living experience.*

If a religion or philosophy doesn't encourage the *personal experience* of Truth then, in my opinion, that system of thought is not worth pursuing. The world doesn't need more intellectuals because it has enough knowledge. It needs more mystics. It's this personal knowing that gives meaning to life because Truth is an *experience,* not a mental abstraction.

Everything in these pages is from personal experience and the events reconstructed from my own private journals. Consider this publication a psychological map to see what stages you have to go through along the way to realization of the True Self.

My wish is for everyone to get an invitation from God.

CHAPTER ONE

AN INVITATION FROM GOD

We have to remember that we originally have our center in God and that without Him, we couldn't exist. Somewhere along the way, though, we made a terrible mistake. We displaced this divine center by putting the ego there and tried to make ourselves into gods, thereby obscuring God as our *natural* center. The purpose of our life on earth is to undermine this unnatural center and re-establish union with the divine.

We don't really live until we realize that Truth is the missing piece that completes our humanity. Everyone on earth is seeking it but doesn't know it because spirituality has been so suppressed that its negative side has surfaced as the most outrageous addictions. Making money, love affairs, the job, drugs, alcoholism, gambling, racing, anything that produces an *intense* sensation is accepted as a substitute but they will never satisfy. The spirit wants the experience of God, not shallow amusements.

Devotion to something higher was always a part of my life but I never thought that God could be known only through religion. I found access to religious ideas only through the psychological understanding of inner experiences, whereas traditional, "churchy" explanations left me high and dry. In my mind, there had to be a more direct and personal way of experiencing the divine and I wanted to know *for myself* whether union with God was possible. I discovered that literature about this numinous experience ranged from confusing efforts to portray it to inconceivable pains to completely deny it, so it seemed that the only way to find out was to practice the spiritual disciplines myself and see what happened. I figured that if they worked for one person, *they should work for everyone.* If results didn't occur then that method wasn't worth pursuing.

Fourth Way disciplines made the most sense. These were practices like remembering yourself, self-observation, body awareness, watching thoughts and feelings, and learning about identification and projection. I found that even though they didn't give instant enlightenment, they at least made daily living more tolerable, so I started practicing self-observation when I was in high school but I don't know why. I just did.

When was 19, I had an experience that stunned my mind because it was such an unknown occurrence. It was late August in Chicago and I was in the back yard reading some mystical book when *I suddenly knew who I was and that I was one with God.* I had the experience of being everything, there was no inner and outer, no separate beings, just God everywhere. I had read about higher consciousness but didn't know that such a state was experientially possible. Reading about a mystical condition and experiencing it was like the difference between reading the notes to a symphony and actually hearing the music.

Nobody could have prepared me for this because my family was Catholic and believed that God existed *out there* and that we were just His lowly creatures, *not* extensions of Himself. I never told my family about this because if I dared to mention that I inwardly experienced God, they would've told me not to talk like that and to have respect for Him. They wouldn't have believed me anyway.

This experience made me see that union with God was attainable *in this life.* I wanted to know if *this* was the mystical experience that spiritual authors wrote about and went from book to book, person to person, to find out if it was. I didn't think that God would produce this happening just for me and wondered if anyone else experienced this, so I made the awful mistake of asking my friends if they had ever experienced anything like this. After watching some of their bewildering reactions, I embarrassingly realized that *nobody knew what I was talking about.* I found that the difficulty in talking about this ordeal wasn't one of semantics but one of experience. No one could relate to what I was describing because no one ever had such a mystical episode happen to him. As far as I knew, the only other accounts of this came from the writings of Indian saints, so I studied Oriental philosophy. I found its literature filled with descriptions of what I was experiencing.

Something in me *sensed* that union with the divine was the goal of earthly life but I couldn't understand why my physical body continued to live if it was. I remember asking myself one day, *"If this is the goal of life, shouldn't I die now?"* That I didn't die right then didn't help one bit because all I got were blank looks and sympathetic smiles from everyone I told this to. Most people thought I was just making it up.

That was when I realized that nobody was interested as to what the purpose of life was. Always wanting to discuss this subject, I used to steer conversations in its direction by casually asking friends if they were interested as to why they were on earth. To my utter amazement, every one of them said "No." I never understood how anyone could be alive and not be interested as to the *why* of it all. I always was.

This experience gave me the inner certainty that no separate person or entity existed, only God. I saw that the division between people and things was imaginary and didn't really exist. The boundary between the inner and outer world was dissolved and there was no longer any inside or outside, just oneness everywhere. There was also a feeling of divine love at this time that didn't come from me because my personal self had seemed to disappear and there was no me in it, just the act of love itself. Not only did this experience let me know that I was one with God but also that *nothing existed but God*. The exterior world to me was like a hologram. Things *seemed* to be happening but, no matter how serious a situation appeared, there wasn't anything to be concerned about. Not really. This state was easily lost when talking or doing any mental work but when my mind wasn't engaged in anything, there was an abiding presence of God within and God without.

The experience faded after about six months and disappeared just as uninvitedly as it came. From then on, my search would be to find out what had happened, why it did and most importantly, how to have it happen again.

I had to make a pilgrimage to another place for that.

CHAPTER TWO

A Shocking Pilgrimage

The next fifteen years were uneventful, filled mainly with jobs, relationships, trying to make a name for myself, and living in the California fast lane. I practiced yoga and meditation and was always on the lookout for a spiritual group to join and kept wishing there was an American group that used everyday language when talking about the spiritual life because most of the ones on the west coast seemed to have an Eastern flavor to them. I always had a hard time relating to Oriental analogies.

I investigated different groups and found one in southern Nevada, so I moved there to be with them and thought that life would be beautiful from then on. I pictured all of us sitting around having pleasant little discussions about Truth and feeling a lot of love for each other. The reality of the situation, however, was quite different.

Nevada is a God awful place and moving to the southern part of that state from the fast lane in California was a severe culture shock. Two things struck me the most upon my arrival. The first was the complete absence of any interest in holistic health in that area and the second was the appalling lack of creativity. I just assumed that both deficiencies were caused by the extreme heat but was never interested enough to pursue their etiologies. There was clearly no sign of intelligence in Nevada.

Nevertheless I was there and eager to start living a *real* spiritual life.

Real Spirituality

I found that spirituality doesn't consist of just sitting around discussing Truth but lies in actually living and practicing Truthful principles. They have to be learned *and practiced* just like anything else in life.

In addition to doing spiritual reading on our own, we attended meetings conducted by a man named Vernon Howard who didn't look spiritual at all. He wore wrinkled clothes and his hair always looked like he just woke up. It seemed like he was forever bawling us out in order to steer us in the right direction and what he said to one person applied to everyone. It wasn't until much later that I realized that his behavior was characteristic of a true teacher, whose only aim is to clean out the students.

The purpose of the meetings was to get rid of all the imaginary concepts we had of ourselves and help us see what we were *really* like underneath our false fronts. This was the initial confrontation with my personal unconscious and with everything that I had been hiding from myself and others. At first I took a lot of what was said as personally insulting. About a dozen times I walked out of the meeting in anger, telling myself that I would *never* return but something kept pulling me back. I felt compelled to keep returning but didn't know why.

We learned that enlightenment doesn't occur by meditating on figures of light but by making the darkness in ourselves conscious and that noticing our dark side is the foundation for any heightening of consciousness. At first this was hard to do because I arrogantly thought that I didn't have any dark features. We were constantly told to snap ourselves out of our daydream state by paying attention to what we were doing at the moment and eventually I understood that we can't awaken simply by *wanting* to do so. Like any other process, spiritual growth needs energy but we waste a lot of it on negative emotions, worry, ner-

vousness, irritability, and daydreaming. The development ·
of consciousness requires attention and inner discipline ·
and we were told to withdraw the energy from one source
so that it could ignite the spiritual potential in another.
The truth about ourselves is a hard thing to take and I
later realized how the meeting between conscious personality and the unconscious has a decidedly disintegrating
effect upon the ego. I had to face unpleasant inner facts
and saw that my parents, teachers, and society never told
me the truth about myself because they didn't know the
truth about *themselves*. Seeing how I had been lied to all my
life by people who didn't know that they were lying to me
made me more determined than ever to know the reality
about what I was like underneath the surface personality.
This became my consuming preoccupation for the next
fifteen years.

We are born with the capacity for God consciousness
but when raised by spiritually unconscious people, we
imitate them and become *just like them*. For example, I was
brought up in a dysfunctional family that considered itself
normal only because everyone else in the neighborhood
had the same neurotic tendencies. If you put 100 people
with the same dysfunctional habits in a room, nothing will
look abnormal to an outside observer since each person is
doing what everyone else is doing. That's how it was in
my case. I imitated the behavior of people who didn't
know that they were teaching me dysfunctional living and
this conduct was reinforced later in life by being around
others with the same bad habits, which led to a lifetime of
rotten behavior. But I discovered that bad conduct wasn't
my real problem.

The central issue was that, like the maladjusted adults I
imitated, *I believed that there was nothing wrong with me.* I
thought that flying into a rage, using filthy words, being
sarcastic and snapping back at people was normal. After
all, everybody else did it. It became obvious that if I didn't
start dancing to a different tune, I'd end up *exactly* where I
was headed.

I needed to change.

CHAPTER THREE

Inner Change Was Necessary

Searching for Truth isn't something that can be occasionally practiced, set aside and then forgotten. It's not a part time hobby but a lifetime pursuit. We either have to be in it all the way or not be in it at all but at the beginning I wasn't ready to devote my whole life to it. I wanted to be spiritual only a few days a week.

We were given spiritual exercises like self-observation, being aware of our bodies, and watching thoughts and feelings so we could become more acquainted with ourselves and slow down the constant churning of thoughts. It was like being a first grader again where everything had to be learned from the beginning, including proper behavior. Compared to the conduct of others in the community, my reactions to daily events were childish and I embarrassingly realized that emotional maturity wasn't one of my strong points. That, too, has to be learned.

There's a spiritual law that says we can't progress to a higher level if we insist on staying on a lower one and I realized that I couldn't simultaneously hang on to self-destructive routines and inwardly advance. I had to choose. Either hold on to the old ways and get nowhere in the spiritual life or let them go. I couldn't have heaven and earth at the same time.

Imagine someone growing up inside a yard with very high walls around it. They are so high that he can't see over them and doesn't know that there's anything beyond. Ever since he can remember, other people have told him that he has to defend the yard for his own protection, so every time a piece of the wall fell off, he'd repair it and fortify it with more cement.

As he grew older, the walls got thicker and the space inside got smaller but this took place so gradually that the man didn't realize that it was happening. Eventually the walls were so thick and the space inside so small that his actions were confined to the smallest movements.

One day a man with insight walks by and urges the prisoner to see that he's not the free person he thinks he is but the trapped man doesn't see his own enclosure. He fiercely resists looking at his walls because that would mean facing the illusion that he's already free but decides to give the outsider a chance. At first he doesn't see any walls because of his overpowering belief that he's already free but as he continues to look, he sees his limitations and how thick they are. The outsider urges the prisoner to notice as much as he can about them, especially about what composes them.

"Don't be afraid to see how trapped you are," he tells him. *"Keep looking at what makes up your prison walls and you'll find they're made of material that you yourself collected. There's something magical about the very act of seeing this."*

And then he vanished.

To his astonishment, the boundaries the prisoner thought were so solid started dissolving and the more he looked, the more transparent the walls became. Finally they disappeared altogether. The man was free and experienced a life without mental limitations.

I discovered that we have certain images of ourselves and these images allow for only a limited number of reactions to daily events. They restrict psychological freedom without our knowing it. The walls are our hardened attitudes and negative beliefs and our reactions are carbon copies of everyone else's. I never questioned whether my behavior harmed others or not and even thought that my negativity gave me personality. One of the hardest things for me to do was to give up the destructive old ways that were killing me because, over the years, I had mistakenly fallen in love with them.

Resistance to inner change can be illustrated with a story.

The Butterfly Farm

Once upon a time there was a boy who raised butterflies. He did this not only for scientific curiosity but also for the sheer pleasure of doing so.

One day he wanted to see if his caterpillars made any sounds when they communicated, so he put a tiny microphone inside their colony and this is what he recorded. Let's listen in.

"We should have an escalator in this place," said one.

"And a wider variety of leaves," mumbled another.

To his astonishment, the boy found that not only could the caterpillars talk but they had a limited number of things they talked about. He discovered that, even though all their physical needs were satisfied, their conversations reflected a feeling of boredom. This baffled him.

One day a butterfly landed on a flower near one of the caterpillars. He said hello but the caterpillar didn't answer. After a few sips of nectar, the butterfly recognized him as a former friend and asked if there was anything he would like to know about inner transformation.

"There is no such thing," the caterpillar replied. *"The way we're born is the way we oughta stay."*

The butterfly was completely bewildered.

"Some of my friends changed," he continued, *"and nobody ever saw them again."* He didn't realize that the winged creature was one of those friends.

The boy found it amazing that there was no two way recognition between them. With continued observation, however, he discovered that his caterpillars suffered from a very peculiar disease.

He found that they were afflicted with "oughtism," a disorder that made them believe they oughta stay the way they were and never change. This condition affected their oughtanomic nervous system and made them dreamily do what they thought they oughta do without ever questioning anything. Their lives became mechanical.

This disorder also blocked their insight to see the connection between the way they thought and what they experienced. Their minds became so lazy that they virtually lost the ability to think for themselves.

But one caterpillar was different.

This one questioned things and the more he did, the more he was able to think for himself. This new way of using his wits reflected itself in his outer activities and his life took on a vitality that none of the other caterpillars had. What's more, he started producing silk on the inside.

The boy knew it was only a matter of time before he had another butterfly.

It's the same with human beings. Without questioning our beliefs, we experience the same situations over and over again and don't realize it. Life loses its freshness and we start wondering where all the spontaneity went.

Looking back on everything, I saw that my life was like a game of badminton and I was the birdie who only imagined that I was in control of the game. One day I came across an article on oughtism that told readers to take a simple test to see if they could be suffering from this dreaded disease, so I did. It went something like this:

1. Do you think you oughta do everything you oughta do?
2. Do you do the things you oughta do just because you oughta do them?
3. Do you sometimes wake up on Saturday with nothing to do and then think you oughta do something?

4. Do you think you oughta be thinking about these things?

I answered "Yes" to all of them and the article said that if I answered "Yes" to *any* of the above questions that I may be living an oughtamatic life. So *that* was my problem, I thought.

I realized that I suffered from oughtism all my life and that it afflicted my whole family but we considered it so normal that we didn't even have a name for it. I did what I thought I oughta do and never questioned anything. Eventually my mind became so listless from nonuse that I heard flapping sounds inside my head on breezy days.

Oughtism prevented me from seeing the connection between the way I thought and my recurring experiences. I spent years thinking that my beliefs were oughtamatically determined by external circumstances. Events came first, beliefs second. Right?

Guess what? It's the other way around.

One disappointment after another made me realize that there was an invisible connection between *what I believed and what happened to me*. The puzzling thing about this is that I found it difficult to give up some of these convictions even though understanding their harm. They'd been a part of me for so long that it was tough to just drop them. It felt too much like leaving behind some old friends.

And guess which one I cherished the most?

It was the notion that I oughta stay the way I was because inner change was scary.

Get this. I thought that if I tampered with my reactions in any way, like refusing to go along with anger, *that I wouldn't be happy anymore*. That's how distorted my beliefs had become because I never questioned them.

Somewhere along the way, though, I realized that oughtamatic thinking wasn't my real problem. Oughtism lingered in my life as long as it did because of another, very unsuspected, condition: *my unawareness of it*.

Picture a man standing inside a circle drawn on the ground. He's been hypnotized and told that he's unable to step outside that circle. He sees people walking around and enjoying life but never goes beyond what he *believes* are his limits. From his standpoint, he feels isolated and left out.

What's the cause of the man's feeling of isolation? Seeing the other people enjoy themselves? No.

It's his unawareness of his own invisible boundaries.

Nothing prevents him from stepping outside that circumference except his unconscious belief that he can't. His thinking mind has been dulled and gullibly accepts a mental impression as an external reality. He believes in imaginary limitations and *experiences what he believes.*

I realized that if I wanted to step outside my present psychological limits, I had to question what I believed. We were told that just as the physical body needs a regular cleansing, so does our belief system and that acquiring new viewpoints will turn our life in a new direction that will be just as real to us as driving down a new highway.

During the meetings, we were told that fear was keeping us from experiencing life the way we wanted to experience it and that the only way to get rid of the fear was to go out and do whatever we were afraid of. To work against one fear is to work against all of them but the *doing of it comes before the fear goes away.* People who refuse to take inner risks live with a feeling of dread that is far more severe than what they would feel if they took the risks necessary to make them less helpless. We not only had to *think* about new behavior but had to actually *practice* it in daily life and were instructed that our actions were critical. We had to *do* something to make our lives match our new attitudes.

I reluctantly conceded that I wasn't the precious little beam of sunshine I thought I was and that I had to learn new ways of thinking. These new attitudes eventually resulted in a change in behavior and I painfully learned that reforming inwardly causes the alienation of so-called friends. This had to happen. Expecting former companions to applaud my new found interest in spirituality was like expecting my best buddies from the bar to celebrate my sobriety. It just wouldn't work.

Eventually life settled down to a regular routine but I only wanted to attend lectures, not do any of the work. Even though we were encouraged to join activities and help out in whatever way we could, there was a lot of ego resistance to following even the smallest instructions. I kept wondering what mopping the floor or throwing out the garbage had to do with spirituality.

We were told that inner healing could only come from going beyond our present limits and were encouraged to practice behavior we weren't familiar with in order to break out of ourselves.

CHAPTER FOUR

BREAKING OUT OF MYSELF

Removing yourself from a self-destructive environment is a necessary first step to overcoming bad influences. Being in a place where the new behavior is encouraged *and practiced* is absolutely essential when starting a new lifestyle. I later understood that the easiest way for inner transformation to occur was to be with others who also wanted to change inwardly.

It's my firm conviction that a certain number of people *must* work together in any spiritual endeavor because one person can do nothing. If several decide to struggle together against psychic sleep, they will wake each other up and it may happen that twenty of them will fall asleep but the twenty first one will be awake and will wake up the rest. So someone who wants to awaken must look for other people who also want to wake up and *work together with them.*

Since the exchange of observations is one of the purposes of any group, *what one experiences is useful to the others.* Suppose ten people got together to learn and work on themselves. They will have ten times more material than just one person working alone and every one of them will be able to use this information. Spiritual seeking doesn't seem so overwhelming when we're in the company of like minded people.

In the community, I found myself among others who weren't of my own choosing and with whom it was difficult to work because of unaccustomed conditions. This created tension but later I understood that this strain was indispensable because it gradually chipped away at our sharp edges. The wider the variety of personalities, the more we see of *ourselves*.

Spiritual disciplines were harder than I realized because they are designed for seeing through the falseness of the ego but realizing this doesn't happen overnight. It's not something that occurs intellectually and we can't just read about how the ego is an illusion and then expect it to disappear. It can only be gotten rid of by practicing behavior that goes *against* it.

An example of anti-ego behavior would be to follow instructions given by someone you just can't stand, going against laziness by volunteering when you don't feel like it, holding your tongue when you want to snap back at someone, and doing exactly what you're told to do even though you have better and more advanced ideas on how to do it.

The more I realized the complexity and diversity of methods for working on myself, the clearer became the difficulties of the way. The immense efforts needed for higher knowledge and the necessity of help became very obvious. I saw that even to begin work on myself in any serious form needed many favorable inner and outer conditions and that starting it offered no guarantee for future results.

The possibility of attaining any spiritual reward seemed so small in comparison with the difficulties that many members lost the desire to make any efforts at all. This was an inevitable stage through which we all have to pass until we learn that it's useless to think of distant achievements. The only thing we can do is consider what we can get done *today* without worrying about how to accomplish something a year from now.

Later I understood that internal unity is obtained by inner fusion and that if a person lives without inner struggle and does whatever he feels like, then he will remain as he is. But if he scrambles with desires that hinder inner development, he then creates an inner fire that will gradually transform his being into a unified whole. My ego knew that this was the beginning of the end for it and it resisted every inch of the way. It didn't give up its domination without a fierce fight and it mentally argued with anyone telling it anything. The struggle against it is the most important part of the work and no further progress can be achieved until this lower self has been worn away.

One of the exercises we were given to practice was not to talk about other people when they weren't present and this, for me at least, was a real eye opener. The purpose was to train ourselves not to gossip and to see how our constant talking was such an unconscious and compulsive act. Many of us realized that when we didn't talk about other people, there wasn't much left to talk about.

There were rules we were told to follow, not only to steer our behavior in the right direction, but to also use them as alarm clocks to help us practice being conscious of ourselves. Bad manners and bad words weren't allowed. Everything was on the honor system, including paying for things when there was no one to take our money. We were all learning good behavior and everyone was an example for everyone else.

There were others before me who dropped out because they wanted to do things their own way and not obey the rules and the thought of being a spiritual failure scared me. I think the only thing that kept me from leaving was knowing that I'd have to spend the rest of my life with the memory of having been defeated by a spiritual discipline. I couldn't handle that.

My decision to stay was shaky at first and although my ego usually ranked high in perseverance, its fortitude quickly disappeared when it saw that other parts of me were bent on its destruction. That's when I started to see that all the virtues I thought my ego possessed were *imaginary*. It was composed of nothing but make-believe qualities and false confidence.

Many times I felt that the spiritual life wasn't for me and that I didn't belong there. It wasn't the heaven I thought it would be because some of the members were obnoxious and not everyone got along with everyone else. Since I had nothing better to do with the rest of my life, I stayed. I changed my attitudes and viewpoints about a lot of things, practiced self-observation and self-remembering. Most of all, I did a lot of praying to God to let me see all the nasty, personal things that I kept tightly concealed from both myself and others. Afterwards, I always asked Him to give me the strength to take it.

I realized that self-observation is done intellectually at first but the deeper you go, the more emotional it becomes. I had to face all the dirty little secrets about myself that I didn't want to admit and look at all the hatred that I picked up and suppressed along the way. We were told that the very first person we'd meet on the way to heaven was the devil but it wasn't until much later that I realized that *the devil was me.*

From the very beginning, we were encouraged to *observe* our negative emotions when they arose but not to *express* them because there was a lot of energy wasted in this behavior. We were told outright to stop blaming other people for *anything* and to give up complaining altogether since both activities were nothing but bad habits masquerading as socially acceptable conduct. Although not able to do either one at first, I found that trying not to criticize or complain made me see how much of each I actually did. Since energy is tangible, negativity is contagious and I found that I always felt lousy after spending time in the company of a negative person but the situation was different in the group. The atmosphere in the community was wonderfully free of negativity and it felt *good.*

As I began to change, I found myself automatically drawn to different kinds of people and did a lot of talking to God at that time and told Him how I felt. Sometimes it was good, sometimes not so good. After about five years, I finally asked Him to give me the desire to devote the rest of my life to Truth and I think He said okay because I remember having a good feeling afterwards.

The days seemed brighter than ever but nobody warned me about the dark nights.

CHAPTER FIVE

First Dark Night: Betrayed By God

Things went all right until the director died. I was confused, lost, without direction and felt that God had abandoned me. The group fragmented and most people went their separate ways but I lingered on for a while. There was no life in the cluster and something was missing but I didn't know what it was at first. Then I realized that nobody talked about God anymore, so I left and kept pretty much to myself. Feeling abandoned by the deity I gave up everything for, I didn't think I could make it on my own but saw no alternative. Most of all, I told myself no more groups.

Until then my spiritual life seemed set in stone but God pulled the rug right out from under me. I had entrusted my life to Him, surrendered a lot of bad practices and resisted impulses to return to the old ways and *this* was how IIe repaid me. He let me down before I even had a chance to prove that I was determined to go all the way for Him and, in my mind, it was the ultimate betrayal.

It took a few months before I was able to consciously admit how much I hated God for bringing me as far as He did and then dropping me. I told Him that no one could pull a dirtier trick than He did and from that point on I was on the side of the devil. At least *he* wouldn't desert me. I wanted to walk away from God the way He abandoned me but I didn't know how, so I made a lot of threats and meant every one of them but underneath all that hatred I secretly cried, *"Why did you do this to me when I gave up my whole life for you?"*

He never answered me.

For the next year, there was a sense of lostness and confusion never before experienced. Other than my job, nothing on the outside really interested me and now there was no interest in God. Life wasn't any good without Him and if spirituality was a gift, it had been taken away. There was no inner direction and I wasn't sure if I could stand on my own. I tried all kinds of distractions, including *lots* of TV, to fill the emptiness and at first these escapes worked but after a while their novelty wore off and they, too, deserted me. I was right back at square one.

I thought that inner fortitude was one of my virtues but nothing prepared me for betrayal by God. The feeling of isolation was so intense that sometimes it felt like I would end up in an asylum from the emptiness, at other times that I would psychologically regress to an animal existence and never recover. The worst part about it was that I thought I'd have to spend the rest of my life in that condition. It felt *permanent.*

During the following year, I never forgave God for what He did but, after a while, the intense hatred decreased and I didn't cry as much anymore. Not wanting to consciously see this hatred was, I think, one of the reasons it was still in me. It took a major upheaval in my life for it to come to the surface and force me to see it after spending a lifetime resisting it.

Knowing in advance that feeling betrayed by God was one of the lessons along the way wouldn't have helped because knowing about it and actually experiencing it are two different things. I saw afterwards that we could never really be abandoned by God and that for an experience to be worth having, it has to *seem* real even though it's not really happening.

The sensation of being betrayed by God shattered me internally and smashed all my previous ways of knowing

Him and let me know that without Him, I was nothing. About a year later, the shattered pieces were drawn together again and rearranged. Now there was a *new* feeling of presence forming inside.

CHAPTER SIX

The Felt Presence

The intense isolation lasted almost a year and afterwards I felt the vague presence of something that wasn't me. It felt strong, like a huge concrete wall and the strange thing about this presence was that I could only *feel* it but not consciously identify it. It was so subtle that I experienced it only as something *not me*. Resisting it was impossible but what it was or where it was taking me, I had no idea.

It seemed that everything was immersed in this presence but it wasn't so much that this energy was in everything but that everything was *in it*. All my attempts to describe it didn't work and I felt that the most sensible thing to do was be quiet and just experience it. Somehow this presence made me know that nothing has a separate existence apart from it or a separate existence of its own.

It came and went in varying degrees for the next two years. Sometimes it was so overwhelming that it was impossible to ignore but the unusual thing about it was that I didn't have to *think* about it for it to be there. It just was. It was a feeling sensation that came from the heart area and it couldn't have been my imagination because you don't imagine feelings. It was always there and I couldn't stop noticing it because I couldn't stop feeling it.

Sometimes it was so strong that I wanted to run outside, grab the first person I saw and yell, *"There IS something else. I know it."* The few people I mentioned this to didn't know what I was talking about but then I didn't give a very good account of it. It was such a new experience that the only way I could describe it was to say that it was an over-whelming *feeling of Presence.* Not much to go on but that's how it felt.

It was like a powerful energy pushing me in a certain direction and went much deeper than what my ordinary mind was used to. The course of action it was urging me to take was obviously the only way to go and it even seemed to have a voice of its own since this was when I started experiencing a voice from the heart area.

I didn't pay much attention to it the first few times it occurred because it seemed to be just another internal happening. The next few times, I noticed that it came from the heart area, not the head, and thought how strange to *feel* a voice. It always came unexpectedly, never talked for very long and most of the things it said were either gentle admonitions or encouraging words.

One time I was working with a metaphysical group to have a local exhibition and volunteered to help staff the booth. It was their first one and nobody knew what kind of turnout it would get. My inner critic started acting up and saying things like, *"What'll you do if nobody stops at the booth? You'll look stupid standing there and the people walking by will laugh at you."* Stuff like that.

When those thoughts went through my head, the voice gently but firmly said, *"Results are not your department. You just do the work."* It let me know that whoever needed to be reached would be reached and that I shouldn't think about results.

Another time I was working on a spiritual project and wanted to resign because it seemed like too much work. The inner voice remarked, *"If you don't do this, somebody else will."* I took this to mean that a certain energy was working itself out on the physical level and that if it didn't come out my body, then it would come out somebody else's. In the inner life, only those who do the work get a spiritual paycheck and it was telling me that *if I wanted the inner reward, I had to do the work.*

The voice lasted a few months and then suddenly stopped. I didn't even know that it ended until one day realized that it hadn't come for a while and afterwards wondered if I did something to offend it or wasn't spiritual enough to keep it. Whatever the reason, it never came again.

I never told anyone about this but another energy started soon after the voice stopped.

Whenever I meditated, there were extraordinary energy pulls from my tail bone and felt like energy shooting upwards to the top of my head. These episodes didn't hurt but they gave me goose bumps along my spine and made me shake, like you do when you're real cold. These pullings also occurred during the day at work and I wasn't always successful at hiding the shaking. Sometimes others would see me shudder and ask, "What's wrong?" and I'd reply that I felt a chill. Most of the time they accepted that.

For the next few months, I sometimes woke up at night and felt intense tingling all over as if I consisted of vibrating magnetic energy, extending out a few feet in all directions. This scared me the first time it happened because I couldn't perceive a definite boundary to my body. Where it ended and everything else began wasn't clear but sort of tapered off without a definite shape. It was a bewildering sensation to watch and although not painful, unnerving since these episodes came only at night. Why they occurred or what they meant, I had no idea.

One night I was lying in bed and felt like I was no longer contained in this body but couldn't say exactly where I was. I didn't seem to be located anywhere and felt as if I extended spherically a few hundred feet on every side. Boundaries between me and everything else disappeared and the sensation continued on and off for a few weeks and then suddenly stopped. Ever since then I could feel cool electricity coming from the palms of my hands and when I hold them close to each other, they're like two magnets where you can feel the attraction and repulsion. It's an interesting sensation but I'm not too sure what to do with it.

I'm firmly convinced that consciousness is a physiological function and that the process of transformation reaches down to the cellular level since the sensations I experienced told me that my whole being was involved, not just the psyche. I believe that changes in either consciousness or in any physical function are experienced reciprocally by both the body and mind. Spirit and matter are the same and the whole person transforms.

Feeling Thoughts

About six months later, I started *feeling* other people's thoughts but when these occurrences came, I refused to acknowledge this ability and chalked it up to coincidence. As these happenings grew in frequency and duration, I had to admit that it was a natural faculty to feel thoughts and as time went on, it increased until all I had to do was be within a few feet of someone and I could *feel* what they were thinking. I would never hear their thoughts, always *feel* them, and not all of them were pleasant either.

Supermarket aisles were my favorite. I could tell what other people were feeling because the aisles are narrow enough that you have to walk within a few feet of each other. One time I passed a lady standing in front of the ice cream case and felt her complaining to herself that the store didn't have the ice cream she liked. I wanted to stop and tell her that it was a shame to waste her energy mentally complaining but I didn't because I also got the feeling that she *enjoyed* complaining to herself.

Very few people knew about this ability. Even though they felt natural, such capabilities were never my aim and not important to me, so I never talked about them. As far as I could tell, they were simply the products of inner development and I didn't care if they were there or not. My goal was higher.

Once its novelty wore off, I didn't pay much attention to this ability and afterwards it slowly disappeared. I have to admit that there was nothing particularly spiritual about these abilities and that they were without any real depth since they neither gave me deeper insight into myself nor taught me anything new about God. They always involved the external world and other people and I initially placed value on these capacities because I thought they came from God. But when they stopped, I couldn't help thinking that I did something wrong or wasn't worthy enough to have them. Much later, I saw that they had nothing to do with Truth and nothing to do with *real* spirituality.

For me, Truth is God and I believe that it's possible to be rid of everything but Truth. We can't possibly lose that. So if these capacities were from God, they should have lasted forever but the fact that they disappeared told me otherwise. I saw that getting caught up in supersensory abilities was to be enslaved by them and I'm now convinced that *all psychic experiences lead to a dead end.* One of the lessons I learned from this was that the ego will do *anything* to ensure its own survival, even put on a supersensory costume and masquerade as an ability from God. Knowing that its days were numbered, this was its next play for survival.

A year after it started, the felt Presence was continuous and stronger than ever. Though it wasn't ecstasy, it made me feel inwardly alive again but this time I was on my own and not part of a spiritual group. It was obviously leading me where *it* wanted to go and couldn't care less whether I chose to go along with its plans or not.

It became increasingly evident that neither I nor any other human being knew the way back to God. Only He knows the way because only He knows the true nature and destiny of His creatures. Our job is to admit that we're lost and let something higher lead us back home. In my opinion, we have two ways to go through life. We could either resist this higher power and cause ourselves a lot of psychological pain or abandon all efforts at self-control

and go peacefully along with it. I chose the second after
experiencing the first.

In either case, it was obvious I'd end up where God
wanted me to regardless of whether I wanted to end up
there or not and sometimes He took me down the scariest
paths to get there.

CHAPTER SEVEN

THE BEGINNING OF THE END

T hree months later, a vague uneasiness set in and I felt possessed by something very evil. It was as if a diabolical force had taken hold of me and was making me do and say the things that *it* wanted but I didn't know what it was or how to get rid of it. Suicidal thoughts were constant and it felt like I didn't have them but *they had me*. For the next few weeks, I felt exhausted and would lie motionless on the bed after work, wide awake but too fatigued to move. There was no energy to do anything.

One night I had a frightening nightmare about demonic possession that was so terrifying I started questioning whether it was really happening and then realized that *I wasn't asleep*. I felt like Mia Farrow in *Rosemary's Baby* when she was raped by the devil and saw that it wasn't a dream. Eventually I calmed down and fell back asleep but then the nightmares changed from visual to tactile.

This time I felt icy fingers of something that I could only describe as death touch my side and their chilly coldness made me jump. Even though I didn't see anything, I felt them and knew that some *thing* freezing cold had touched me. If demonic possession and the sensation of icy cold fingers didn't really happen, then for the first time I had lucid nightmares.

The next morning, the exhaustion was gone and whatever possessed me for the previous weeks had delivered its communication the night before and vanished. I believe that the unconscious always sends symbolic messages in advance concerning any major psychological event and think that the lucid nightmare of death was a premonition of something inwardly about to happen.

A week after the death nightmare, I was lying in bed and was suddenly jolted by a sensation that felt like something inside my head had abruptly shut off. Afterwards, I saw that there was only stillness and emptiness inside, nothing else, and then realized that the ego, the sense of personal self, was no longer there. It was gone.

This was such a shock that all my thoughts unexpectedly stopped and there was no internal movement at all. From this experience, I *knew* that the self was not a person or entity and didn't really exist. The stunning nature of the episode lasted about a week but the realization that the ego was not a real entity continued from then on.

It was quite a jolt to have lived with a sense of I, me and mine for almost half a century and then find out that it was all a gigantic hoax, a colossal case of mistaken identity. I felt confused and bewildered as to what had actually happened and withdrew from everyone. More than anything else, though, I wanted to talk to someone about this but didn't because I had made that mistake before. No one would've believed me anyway.

My emotional capacities diminished over the next few months and felt like they were shutting off. Intellectual faculties that had operated on fast forward slowed to practically a complete halt and just the act of thinking seemed to required more energy than I had. It felt like I was inwardly dying.

The insight that the ego was not an entity seemed to be two things at once. First, it was the revelation of a mistaken belief and second, the opening of a deeper center, which felt as if it replaced the ego's position as the nucleus of my life. I don't know what the source of the ego energy was that shut off but it seemed to be some kind of reflecting mechanism of the mind that allowed it to bend and see *itself*, and I realized that this was what produced the illusion of a separate self. It made sense that if the mind didn't see *itself*, there would be no it-*self* and this duplicating action accounted for the feeling of a separate me. I want to emphasize that the opening of a deeper center was a *stunning* experience, *not* an ecstatic one. It stopped all mental processes because something not of the mind had infiltrated and broken into it, leaving an empty sensation as if somebody I had been living with for a long time suddenly left. There was a feeling of no life, no energy, and no sense of self, just a lot of *dead air* inside. The hardest part about this was that I felt there was nothing I could do about it.

A few months later, I realized that the life cycle of the ego was controlled by something *outside* itself but we don't see this until *after* it ends, like having a dream and not knowing it's not real till it's over. Similarly with the illusion of a separate self. We don't see the deceptive nature of the ego while living with it, only *after* it's been completely lived through.

But I think there is a way to speed this up.

CHAPTER EIGHT

SPEEDING UP THE PROCESS

I t's my belief that increased consciousness eliminates the need for constant repetition of experiences and that the more conscious you are of occurrences, the more benefit you get from them. The more benefit you get, the fewer the number of repetitions needed. The problem is that most people think that they are *already conscious* and so never investigate why they keep finding themselves in the same situations. They don't know that they can eliminate repeating the same experiences by becoming conscious of *everything* in their lives, *including becoming conscious of how unconscious they really are.*

In my opinion, the ego is seen for the error it is after it's lived through all the experiences it needs but I always wondered why Eastern philosophy says that it takes hundreds of lifetimes to do this. I think it's just as valid to believe that it can be done away with in one lifetime as it is to believe that it needs a plurality but how many it takes is not the issue. The real concern is whether we can completely live through it in *this* life.

We are told that some people have to go through the same experiences because it takes them longer to "get it" than it takes others but I never really accepted that. Nobody ever satisfactorily explained to me *why* everyone didn't "get it" right away and eventually I learned not to rely on other people for answers. It was obvious from the empty look in their eyes that they were just as lost as I was.

My explanation is that the degree of consciousness determines whether or not we need to experience something again and that we repeat an experience only if we're not *completely conscious* of it the first time. *Consciousness is everything.* It gives a vividness to an experience that it would not ordinarily have and lets us feel everything about it. The more conscious we are, the wider our field of reception and the wider the range of impressions received during an experience, the fewer the number of repetitions needed in order to learn the lesson.

My own experience with different spiritual exercises showed me that consciousness is actually made up of three component skills that become integrated into a larger one. Once these individual components are learned, they become automatic and blend into the smooth flow of consciousness. But as in acquiring any new skill, the initial learning is often a struggle, first with each component skill and then with their smooth integration.

As each is practiced, it merges with the one previously learned until, one day, you're conscious, just as one day you found yourself driving without thinking about it. It becomes automatic and continuous and, in time, you almost forget that you had to *learn* to be conscious, just as you almost forget that you had to learn to read and walk. But once you have learned to read, you know how to read for life, you know how to walk for life, and once you've learned to be conscious, you experience consciousness for life. You don't have to go on forever adding additional basic skills because from then on, progress takes the form of practice.

These three individual components of consciousness are: self-observation, self-remembering, and noticing projections.

Self-Observation

I think it's important to realize that we live in a sort of waking hypnotic state of mind where our eyes are open and our bodies are moving around but our minds are a million miles away. Self-observation consists of watching your physical movements, being aware of your thoughts and noticing whatever feeling is going through you. All you do is watch yourself just as if you were observing someone else.

In self-observation, you don't judge, criticize or comment on anything you see in yourself. You observe the way you walk, the tone of your voice, the size of the room you are in, what you are thinking or feeling. You don't try to get rid of or change anything you see, you just watch. Self-observation does not have anything to do with *thinking* about yourself. Thinking always involves mental chatter but self-observation is a wordless action. Non-verbal. Thoughtless.

Try it right now. Stop reading for a minute and become aware of the position of your body, your feet on the ground, the temperature in the room, the background sounds, what your hands are doing, whether the muscles in your face are tense or relaxed. Do you see the difference between the self-absorbed state you were in when you started reading this and the one now? Did you also notice that thought *temporarily stopped* when you observed yourself? In the former state, you had no awareness of either yourself or your surroundings but now you do.

Self-observation is seeing your inner state at the same time that you watch whatever is happening in the outer world. It's a *new way of using the mind* and an exercise that can be done at work, at home or waiting for a bus but persistence pays off. Practice it as much as you can because this state can be made *permanent* with practice.

Self-Remembering

This is an exercise that is easy to explain but difficult to do. It's the act of simply keeping the *feeling* of your existence in consciousness as much as possible. When you're walking from one room to another, talking to someone, driving the car, anything at all, be aware that *you* are walking, talking, driving. You don't think about yourself but just keep the nonverbal feeling of I in everything you do.

Experience shows that actually doing this exercise is not the hard part. It's *remembering* to do it. The mind is so used to operating on automatic with no one in the driver's seat that it's difficult to do at first. Eventually you realize that you are not conscious of your own existence and come to the startling conclusion that unconsciousness has been your normal state up till now.

Self-remembering initially requires a mental effort but it gets easier with practice. You will be able to remember yourself for longer periods until, one day, you find that you automatically remember yourself all the time and the feeling of I will be in everything you do. You will have started the mechanism of *self* consciousness.

After a while, the two practices of self-observation and self-remembering merge into a single act and result in direct sensory perception without thought interference. It's like having awareness focused on two things at once, the external or internal impression and the realization that *you* are experiencing it. It's the *feeling* of I combined with an observation.

I realized after practicing this that every impression we receive is filtered *through the ego* and that we never see anything without contamination by personal thoughts. Self-observation combined with self-remembering is *awareness without thought* and so bypasses interference by the ego. The two exercises combined are an effective way of controlling thoughts and, in my experience, constitute the basic components of consciousness.

I used to think how wonderful it would be to experience sensory awareness without any self-reference like the animals do because without a self, someone could make an unkind remark and there would not be any hurt feeling since there would be no one there to refer it to. Self-observation and self-remembering are shortcuts to an undisturbed mind.

Noticing Projections

Picture a circle containing all your character traits. It's divided in half and on the right side are all the qualities you like and consider to be part of you and on the left are all the ones that you don't like and have either ignored or suppressed. But just because you don't like the traits on the left doesn't mean you no longer have them. You can't get rid of any human trait any more than you can cut off your head because the psyche has a universal structure common to everyone just like the body does.

In the psychological world, out of sight doesn't mean out of mind and whatever you are unconscious of gives it free reign to grow beneath the surface completely unchecked. In other words, if you don't know about your unseen traits then you don't have them, *they have you.* Anything you are unconscious of has that much more power over you *because you don't know about it.*

These disowned traits are your "lost" parts and contrary to popular belief, don't contradict the conscious personality but *complement it.* Most things in the unconscious are pure gold and anything in the unconscious will be useful and good when it's made *conscious.* But since all traits have a bipolar nature, characteristics that look immoral or embarrassing to the ego are only the complementary side of a valuable energy. Believe it or not, you will never feel complete without these lost parts.

Finding them can be illustrated with a story.

The Missing Diamond

Once upon a time there was a lady who owned a set of 100 interconnecting diamonds. Each one was uniquely cut from the same stone and fit in perfectly with the others. The collection was so intricately designed by a Master Diamond Cutter that there wasn't another one like it in the world. It was her prized possession.

One day she discovered that a piece was missing. The lady went from room to room and searched the whole house, turning on the all lights and moved every bit of furniture. The lost diamond was nowhere to be found. She grew weary after not finding it and fell into deep despair.

"It's hopeless," she thought. *"The set's just not complete without that missing piece."*

As she was looking out the window one evening she caught a glimpse of something bright reflected on the glass. She looked to see where it was coming from. There, in the middle of the floor, was the missing diamond.

"I looked in that spot a hundred times," she mumbled.

But it didn't matter. The relief of finding the absent piece made her forget all her previously unproductive efforts. Her collection was complete again.

Our psychological parts are like a unique set of diamonds cut from a larger one but we have to be aware of all the segments in order to have a complete collection. Psychologically, the out-of-sight diamond represents any part of ourselves that we're unaware of. These fragments are "lost" to consciousness but we can rediscover them by becoming *aware* of them. It's an adventure in self discovery.

Somewhere along the way, though, we made a dreadful mistake because we *identified* with certain characteristics and this led to the exclusion of many of our qualities that could have been numbered with the others. Those rejected traits were the ones that were pushed underground and became our "lost" parts. We forgot about them and cultivated other socially acceptable traits.

But contrary to common belief, *overdeveloped qualities become stumbling blocks to wholeness* instead of building blocks. Overdevelopment of some features always means the underdevelopment of others and, as a result, your continued psychological growth is impaired because many of your attributes remain unconscious. And unconscious means undeveloped.

The curious fact about your unknown traits is that everyone sees them *except you*. Your friends know about them and strangers see them right away but here is where projection comes to the rescue.

Projection is a psychic activity that occurs whenever an unknown aspect of yourself sees itself in somebody else. Whatever you don't know about yourself is *always noticed in other people first*. If an unconscious trait is projected, you see it outside yourself as though it belonged to someone or something else but it's important to remember that *everything unconscious is projected*. It does not necessarily have to be a person who is the recipient either. Pets, cars and bank accounts can also hold projections.

Your inner self knows what needs to be made conscious but if you are not used to looking within, it does the next best thing. It "projects" the unknown quality onto other people as if it says, *"Look. You need to know about this trait but if you don't look **inside** and see it, you'll have to see it on the outside."*

A good way to recognize a projection is to notice what you like and dislike in others. Being fascinated by another person is a good indication that you are projecting a quality that is in *you* onto someone else and the converse is true. If you just can't stand somebody for some reason then you have the disliked feature in *you* but don't know it. You notice it someone else but its origin is in *you*.

One of the most difficult exercises for me to do was to deliberately watch a videotape of police brutality and see that all the cruelty exhibited on the tape was also in *me*. I always found brutality repulsive and thought that it was something I was incapable of but upon closer inspection, it was my self-righteous ego that considered itself above malevolence. I realized with the deepest humility that, since I found the activity so repulsive and thought that I completely lacked the trait, I had refused to see it *in myself* and projected my own unadmitted cruelty onto others. It took a few months before I was able to admit that all the savagery that I saw acted out in the videotape was also *in me* and much later understood that cruelty is a feature typical to all humanity, the only difference being that some people externalize it more than others. It's my experience that those who deny the presence of any malevolent traits in themselves are usually the ones who act them out the most vehemently but don't know it. Cruelty is *always* unconscious.

It's a psychological law that *you always see your own denied faults in others* and proving this is easy. Just notice the next time you have an argument with someone. Take a look inside and see if you possess the very things you're accusing the other person of. If you're honest, you'll find that you do.

Underneath the surface, human beings are not as nice as we imagine them to be but we naively assume they are because we project our fantasy self-images onto them. By doing this, we create a whole series of imaginary relationships based essentially on our projections and these illusory assumptions make up the starry-eyed foundation of human relationships, which swarm with unrealistic ideas of how we *imagine* other people to be.

Every person who is not introspective is bound to his environment by a whole series of projections and is completely unaware of the compulsive nature of his relationships. Projections are charged with emotion and the only way to be free of them is through conscious recognition and to realize that what you are projecting is in *you*. You see others in the same way that you see yourself and what you don't see in yourself, you don't see in others. All the features that you see in other people are really *personified versions of your own personality*.

The majority of human beings feel no obligation to make these projections conscious even though they are dangerously fraudulent. Take falling in love, for example. Most romantic relationships end bitterly because the lovers see only the qualities they want and need the other to have but, after a while, the paint wears thin and each sees what the partner is really like underneath the dreamy costume. Unrealistic projections always contain the essence of their own destruction.

I've observed that human beings at their present spiritual level have a minimum of self-awareness combined with a maximum of attachment to other people and external objects. The irritating thing about noticing projections is the conviction that if everybody did it, the world would be a better place to live but to do it ourselves, on the other hand, is a different story. We would have to demand of ourselves, and no one else, all the things that we habitually require of others and have to handle the job of self-owning all the deviltry that we so blatantly attribute to the people down the block. After all, it's a lot easier to have an enemy that we can point to and blame everything on than it is to take responsibility for everything in *ourselves.*

This puts a brand new meaning on the phrase wherever you go, there you are because what you really see "out there" is *yourself.* The issue here is to recognize the real source of the features you see in others, which is always in *you,* but the good news is that once a projection is recognized, it can be withdrawn. This action returns the energy to its rightful owner and you begin to understand what belongs *to* you by seeing what comes *from* you. This is especially important for self-knowledge because then it's simply a matter of using other people as mirrors to see what *you* are really like underneath.

So the rule of thumb is this: *Any person or object that carries a projected image will either attract or repel you.* Projections are so highly charged with emotional energy that they act like a powerful magnet to either pull you toward someone or push you away. Keep in mind that you project *everything* that is still unconscious and that whatever quality attracts or repels always exists in *you,* never in someone or something else. Imaginary barriers are dissolved by becoming aware of what is already inside and your aim is to become so free in spirit that it no longer matters whether or not you have the people and things you crave.

Be a people watcher and try to see at least one aspect of yourself everyday in someone else. When you see more of yourself, you move out of what feels comfortable and your whole life expands to take in more of what there is to experience. As you go through the day, be aware of where you find yourself hesitating or cringing at seeing something and start planning your future risks based on these observations. Remember that the more you see of *yourself*, the more whole you become.

As you continue to watch, you will become more acquainted with aspects of yourself you probably were not aware of before. This is good. Keep in mind that the very process of exposing so-called bad aspects to consciousness *transforms* them and the level of your being rises. You are bringing to light all the things that previously operated in the dark and as you practice, you'll find that many of the former things that bothered you don't hit you with the same intensity as before.

You are starting to become *free* and reach beyond your present self.

CHAPTER NINE

REACHING BEYOND THE SELF

I saw that my identity consisted only of beliefs and mental ideas about myself and that these concepts were only thoughts *about* myself. They don't prove the reality of a separate self but the fact that only a few people question the validity of a separate existence shows what a powerful hold this deception has on the psyche. Not only does this illusion provide false inner security and shaky self-confidence but acts as an effective barrier to unity consciousness.

The first step to going beyond the ego is to see through the boundaries of personal thoughts and memories that give the tricky feeling of having a separate existence. By dropping self identifications and mental notions of who you *think* you are, you create an inner vacancy that allows something higher to enter. Gradually, you become who you really are when you stop being who you *think* you are. To put it another way, in order to experience wholeness, you have to stop believing you're separate from the whole.

You create this inner void by disassociating from all concepts of yourself and letting go of identifications with your body, your thoughts, feelings, self images about being a good father, a loving mother, a friendly neighbor, an efficient employee, a spiritual seeker. It can never be emphasized enough that you are not any thoughts about yourself because the real you is beyond thought and not something that can be thought about. I found that whenever I used my mind to shape my understanding of God, I wrongly concluded that I "knew" Him and began to predict what He could and couldn't do for me. Much later, I discovered that spirit is an experience, *not a mental abstraction.*

So what will happen to you when you give up your notions about yourself?

It will feel like an inner death takes place but what passes away is everything that supported a false sense of identity and make-believe feeling of security. It's important to remember that when identifications are dropped, there is no self that disappears because there was no entity there to begin with, only thoughts and memories that made up the only self you knew. A shaky one, at that.

Letting go of a lot of imaginary stuff is the initial step to inner freedom because you have to sacrifice what you imagine you have in order to have something real. Before you can walk hand in hand with the newness of a real self, you have to first be free of the old self, the mental self, and it's comforting to know that amid all this inner housecleaning you can't lose anything that is part of the essential Self. Truth won't allow it. You never have to worry about throwing the baby out with the bath water because only the unreal can be dropped and the sooner the better.

But we seem to have a problem here. Since the ego can't go beyond itself, how can this state be reached? This is done by seeing that the mental boundaries you believe constitute a separate self don't actually exist. Your collection of personal memories does not ensure the existence of a separate self but gives the convincing illusion of having one.

Trying to think your way into a real existence won't work because thought can't go beyond itself. A higher perception is needed, that of awareness without thought. Attempting to use the ordinary mind to reach something higher than itself is like running from one corner to another in a stalled elevator. There is a lot of inner activity but no upward movement.

The search for our authentic identity can be illustrated with a story.

Whimsical Valley

Once upon a time there was a town called Whimsical Valley. It was a theatrical place where everyone pretended to be all sorts of different characters. They all enjoyed playing various roles just for the fun of it.

A man on one side of town imagined himself to be a knight in shining armor. A woman on the other side of the city idealized herself as a damsel in distress and their appropriate roles drew them together. Still others fancied themselves as heavenly messengers with a mission to save the world. Everyone relished playing a certain personality one day and something else the next.

But after a while their amusement turned into monotonous drudgery.

The people of Whimsical Valley performed their different parts for so long that they started *believing* in their starry-eyed roles. They found it harder and harder to remove their disguises at night and their masks started sticking to their faces. Many left them on while they slept because it hurt too much to take them off.

One day a wise magician was passing through town. He saw that the people had trouble removing their masks so he went to the local paper and took out an ad for a free demonstration of his *Miracle Mask Remover*.

"No sticky sprays or messy powders," the ad read. *"Guaranteed to remove masks with continued application."*

Almost everyone in Whimsical Valley saw the ad but only a few showed up. The magician understood that most had grown so accustomed to their masks that *they no longer believed that they wore them*. He knew that they didn't think his presentation held anything in it for them.

On the night of the exhibition he passed out free samples of the mask remover and instructions on how to apply it. He urged the attendees to become aware that they were acting from fictitious ideas about themselves and explained to them that they were too *identified* with the parts they played.

"You've worn your masks for so long," he said, *"that you don't even know you have them on anymore. But if you practice these instructions everyday,"* the magician continued, *"your masks will eventually fall off."*

And then he vanished.

Some of the people felt that the wise man had a good product but weren't convinced that they themselves wore false faces. They took their bottles home and never opened them and continued to act out the roles of their masks, all the while *believing* that they were being themselves. They even went around telling others in Whimsical Valley that the magician was a fraud.

Others who attended the demonstration tried the mask remover. Some forgot to use it everyday because it was a new activity for them but they kept at it. It wasn't until their masks started coming loose that they were even able to believe that they wore them. Eventually their masks became so unattached that they fell off by themselves.

One by one, the brave people who practiced the magician's instructions took great delight in rediscovering their authentic features. Each one knew that this was the familiar appearance he used to know and felt nothing but gratitude for the wise man's visit. He helped them return to what they originally were.

Over the years, I have formulated three simple rules to keep in mind for reaching beyond the ego.

The first is that there's nothing for you to *do*, only something to *understand*. It's important to remember that your genuine features are mixed in with a lot of *acquired identifications* of what you think you should be. You are not your physical body, your personality, thoughts, feelings, home, career, bank account or any concepts you have of yourself. You are just as different from these things as you are from the clothes you put on in the morning.

When you get rid of false identifications, some areas of your life that previously seemed to fit will stop fitting. Shifts in taste and perception frequently accompany shifts in identity. One of the clearest signals that something healthy is afoot is the impulse to weed out, sort through and discard old clothes, papers, and belongings.

Half your wardrobe will start to look funny. You may decide to reupholster a couch or just toss it out. Musical bents will alter. There may even be bursts of spontaneous singing and dancing. In short, your real tastes and personal identity will start to emerge.

What you have been doing is wiping your inner mirror. Up till now, there's been a blur between you and your real self but as you drop identifications, your image becomes clearer and it may surprise you. You will discover likes and dislikes that you had not acknowledged.

A fondness for ivy. So why do you have those cactuses? A dislike for brown. No wonder you never felt right wearing that earth tone sweater. Conditioned as we are to accept other people's definitions of us, this emerging individuality can seem like self-will run riot. It isn't.

The second is not to assume you already know everything there is to know about yourself. There is a lot more comprising your entirety than you realize. Thinking that you presently understand yourself is like gazing at the tip of an iceberg and taking for granted you have seen the whole thing. In actuality, most of what you do and say is determined unconsciously.

Most of your behavior, for example, has been learned by unconsciously imitating others. People are strange. It's as if we have an inborn mechanism that automatically makes us *imitate* anything we see or hear. Believe it or not, almost everything you do is because you saw somebody else do it first.

I did an experiment once to see if others could be influenced to behave differently without their knowing it and gave it a time limit of one month. Everyday I repeated the same nonsensical gestures over and over again while talking with them.

Guess what?

Before the month was up, two others were already performing rudimentary versions of my silly displays. This confirmed my suspicion that people will unconsciously imitate any behavior *as long as they see somebody else do it first.* But seeing how easy it was to influence others didn't prepare me for the stunning conclusion from this experiment. The unexpected eye-opener was that if I wanted others to change their behavior, *I had to first change mine.*

Why?

Because people can't perform a new behavior until someone first *shows* them what it looks like. Once they see how it's done, they will *automatically mimic* this fresh conduct without question. *Imitate what you see* seems to be one of the laws of the unconscious.

Finally, realize that no person or circumstance can stop you from experiencing this natural state. Your innate self is something you can enjoy in this life right here on earth. It's a rediscovery of what you essentially are and not a rare occurrence reserved for a privileged few. It's an interior growth into spiritual maturity.

With patience and persistence, you will start realizing who you are and, more importantly, *what you're not.* Understand that you don't need to start from anywhere than where you are right now and that no sincere effort on your part is ever wasted. Begin with the thought that having just a little bit of light leads to more light. It always does.

No one goes to a king and asks for a penny. Now try applying this same principle to your inner life and ask God to let you experience your genuine nature from one end to the other. Just request a lot and you'll get a lot.

The more you practice noticing how identified you are with people and objects, thoughts and feelings, the more pleasant life will become but it's not the outside world that is changing. It's *you.* You'll be surprised at how much energy you still have at the end of the day because it was not wasted by useless thoughts and unconscious identifications.

So practice every day. At first it will be hard to remember because the mind is used to its habitual sleepy state. Up till today it has operated on automatic but now you are training it to perform a new function. Don't worry that you may not be able to do it at first. Just keep trying. A new and authentic sense of existence will fill the vacancy as your mind becomes empty of all notions of a separate self. You will go from thinking about who you are to knowing *that* you are.

CHAPTER TEN

SECOND DARK NIGHT:
ABANDONED BY GOD

A fter the opening of the deeper center, I saw that the ego can only be known in retrospect by its *absence*. Everything I believed about it in the past turned out to be only partially true because *I didn't see it for the illusion it was while living in it*. Only after it disappeared did I realize what it was by its nonpresence.

The falling away of the ego center was the experience of inner emptiness and the sensation of losing God. It left me in utter darkness and feeling as if the core of my being had suddenly dropped out. Without God I had no sense of self and without a sense of self, I had no sensation of God.

When the ego fell away, all its ambitions, desires, energies, interests, inclinations, emotional reactions, and all of its experiences of God vanished. Factual memories remained but the *feelings* associated with these memories faded and I realized that when the ego shut off, any experience in which it invested *itself* went with it.

Even though the greatest insight I ever had was that union with God is more precious than all other experiences put together, I painfully learned that *without a sense of self, there was no sense of God*. If the self is the entity experiencing God and the self disappears, then who's left to encounter

67

God? When there's no one to be aware of the divine, the divine seems to vanish.

This ordeal was accompanied by a sense of being lost to myself and by a greater sense of having lost God. It's important to point out that, until the ego fell away, the only self I knew was the personal ego self. It was the ego that put all of its energies into the pursuit of a spiritual life and all my experiences of God were screened *through it*. Even the most mystical of them were tainted with a sense of self and I realized that all my attempts to find Truth were ultimately self-centered. My ego had gone in search of God and attached itself to Him through ascetic means because it wanted Him for *itself*.

After the ego began to shut down, everything felt dead and all my actions seemed hollow and without meaning. There seemed to be no purpose to existence anymore and nothing interested me. Just going to work every day required a superhuman effort and I wanted to walk away from it all. There was no satisfaction in anything because there was no self to *feel* satisfied and the absence of God left a big hole in my life. I kept wishing I could experience It again.

The sensation of deadness inside felt like it would go on forever. The felt Presence had disappeared because that, too, was the divine experienced *through the self* and the emptiness within made the most fleeting sensation seem like an eternity. It felt like another dark night of the soul coming on.

A short time later, I again told God how much I hated Him for abandoning me and that I hoped He was having a lot of fun dealing out some beautiful experiences and then disappearing. But this time it was different. I couldn't cry because now there wasn't much of a self left to cry and this time there wasn't any extreme emotional reaction, just a deep sense of emptiness. A big, blank *nothing*. I learned that when there's not much of a self to *feel* abandoned, the abandonment doesn't hurt so much.

I thought that the annihilation of the ego was the lowest I could go but it wasn't. The ego's shattering was just the *beginning* of its breakup, or rather its break-in, by the divine and the bottom was nowhere in sight. The emptiness was deeper than I imagined and felt like an extreme stillness, an unearthly calm. The strange thing about this peacefulness was that it seemed to want to go *outward*, for what I wasn't sure.

The downhill slide in energy continued for the next half year, accompanied by the feeling that there could not be any lower point than this but there always was. I kept asking myself, *"How far down does this emptiness actually go?"* Finally, eight months later, it felt like all inner psychic life was drained and all I saw was nothingness inside and out. I knew I had hit rock bottom.

The experience of God was now only a memory and there seemed to be an abrupt and baffling dead end. Any certitude of an inner life had disappeared and I felt like a spiritual flatliner since writing about inner experiences no longer interested me. My mental faculties seemed dead and I painfully learned that when the experience of God disappears, *so does the desire to serve Him.*

There was complete absence of energy and it was a major effort for a few weeks just to move the body around. Not only was the emptiness getting stronger but more difficult to come out of. It felt heavy and hard to escape from. Sometimes I would lie in bed, totally conscious but unable to move or even keep my eyes open for long. Something inside had come to a complete end and, quite honestly, I could not understand how my physical body remained alive. With no energy and a feeling of being completely abandoned by God, I saw no way forward. No matter how hard I prayed for help, He never answered.

There was a physical body that was moved around by external forces but no self anymore the way I had known one. My mind tried to revive old habits but nothing worked and after a while I got used to the inner vacancy. I no longer expected anything to come and fill it.

The absence of energy lasted almost six weeks but at the time it happened, I didn't understand it to be the final death of the old self. It was quite a bewildering sensation to have no energy, no clear sense of self, no experience of God and no inner life that I knew of. I told myself that if I had to live the rest of my life in that condition, I didn't want to live at all.

There was a complete loss of interest in anything, including spirituality, and upon closer inspection I found that when the ego shut down, along with it went all the things that gave me a sense of identity. I learned that I could lose *everything* and life went on just as it did before but now there was a feeling of lostness and especially of directionlessness. There wasn't even an interest in finding Truth anymore.

I always assumed that the passing away of the old nature would be accompanied by fear and was more afraid of feeling the fear than of the dying itself. Out of curiosity and fascination, I wanted to know what it was like to *consciously* experience inner death and thought it would be a disturbing ordeal but it was not. More than anything else, I was especially baffled as to why God didn't bother to send help after I had given up so much for Him. It was only afterwards that I understood that inner death had to be experienced *completely alone* because if anyone or anything had saved me, it wouldn't have been a death.

A few weeks later the emptiness was still there but there wasn't any fear, just a feeling of no life and no energy. After watching my own disappearance, I thought that something would immediately rush in to fill the vacancy but when nothing happened right away, I started wondering just how long this dying process would take. In contrast to the ego life of activities and ambitions, the emptiness was quite bewildering. I knew that to try and fill it would be useless and it seemed that the only thing to do was let the inner vacancy be there for as long as it wanted. I saw no alternative.

One Sunday I wanted to know just how much of this emptiness I could stand to examine and was surprised to find that there was no boredom at looking at my own nothingness. The more I reflected on why there wasn't any dreary feeling accompanied with viewing nothing, the

more I realized that boredom can't exist without a self to
feel bored.

Mental activity seemed to slow to a complete halt and
there was a lot of inner silence without a sense of self.
Thoughts about I, me, and mine were virtually nonexistent
and even though I still used the word I, it had lost its
former meaning. There wasn't much ambition to do anything without a clear perception of self and I realized that
whatever happened to me inwardly from now on was
completely up to God. It was obvious that, come what
may, He was going to do what needed to be done *with my
consent or without it.*

The passing of the old nature was so silent and so
undramatic that I didn't even know it was gone until it
was all over and it was only in retrospect that I understood
this as the final stage of the ego. Not only was my whole
life of believing in myself a fantastic mental deception but
my own inner death—something that I had looked forward to—was a no-nothing experience. Afterwards I saw
that what we call death is only a very quick and *impercep-
tible passage* from one state to another and that this moment
is unknown to consciousness.

The self's death was *nothing* and there was no fear, just a
feeling of no life and no energy, and the precise moment of
its happening wasn't noticed. Later I realized that there is
no such thing as the *experience* of death, only continuous
transformation, and felt the immortality of life but it
wasn't *my* immortality. It clearly belonged to something
else.

It surprises me that people say they believe in an after-
life and yet are afraid of dying but what amazes me even
more is that they don't realize that in order to be born
again, they first have to experience the *death of their former
self.* Cessation of the old self first, birth of the new second.
It *has* to come in that order. The new birth is overempha-
sized to the point where the necessary disappearance of
the old is completely overlooked.

Once we have been through the first *inner* extinction,
there's a feeling-knowing of our own immortality. Going

through a spiritual dissolution while the body is still alive
lets us *know* that death is not the end but only a word arbitrarily given to a certain point in transformation. Experiencing immortality *while still on earth* is no longer something we intellectually agree with but inwardly *feel*.

Seeing nothing inside at this time let me know that my
inner life was completely up to a higher power and that it
was pure imagination to think that I had any say in the
matter. If there were to be no future experiences of God,
then that's the way it had to be. Nothing was up to me
anymore because *there was no longer any me* for anything to
be left up to.

I learned that every movement to a higher level is
always preceded by an inner crisis and by what appeared
to be my world coming to an end. Everything that seemed
to support my spiritual life was completely undermined
and there was a feeling of abandonment so intense that I
told God from that point on I wanted nothing more to do
with spirituality.

In the meantime, though, the issue at hand was the
strange disappearance of God as an *external deity* and this
terrified me because I couldn't imagine living without
dependence on an exterior power. There was a little altar
in my bedroom that I used as a place of veneration and the
sense of divinity was disappearing from that, too. What
scared me the most, however, was the thought that if there
was no higher power then my entire spiritual life was
nothing but a gigantic head trip, a personal delusion of
such immensity that I was afraid it would push me to the
edge of my sanity.

The absence of God outside me was so alarming that I
told myself I'd had it once and for all with His disappearing acts. I experienced such a violent emotional reaction to
His external withdrawal that I took down the altar, threw
it away and slammed the door so hard the windows
shook. Afterwards I just sat there, waiting for the rest of
my inner life to collapse.

It felt like God had pulled out completely and that this
whole spiritual business was nothing but a big joke. The

feeling of being dropped was intense but this time there was no entity doing the abandoning and no me being abandoned, *only the feeling*. There were no actors, divine or otherwise, and I felt caught between a rock and a hard place. I had nowhere to run except to just sit there and feel the pain.

So I sat and waited. And waited. And when I thought my spiritual life was completely over, there was the flash of a realization that God was *inside* me. It was gone in an instant but it was *real* and it let me know that the divine had to first completely remove itself from the outside so it could reappear later on the inside. I was so relieved that I didn't know whether to be mad or happy. It felt like a divine trick was played on me and the consolation prize was God Himself.

Realizing that there's no outside power to depend on was quite a shock but a necessary one to go through in order to be able to stand inwardly alone. A few nights later, I dreamt that a man was shot and everyone in the room deliberately waited until his life energy was completely gone before calling for help. Upon reflection, it made sense that the old self had to be thoroughly emptied before the new inner essence arrived.

In retrospect, I saw that my altar only held a divinity projection for me and the withdrawal of this projection seemed like God was disappearing on the outside. During the following year, the inner feeling of the divine increased and I found that I was not interested in having an altar anymore. I didn't need to project Him onto anything because It was becoming an *inner reality*. It's experiences like these that let me know that we could never really throw God out of our lives, no matter how hard we tried.

It seemed natural to think that I had fallen out of favor with God when things didn't happen the way I expected and it took me a long time to see that this irrationality was due to my own lack of understanding. The ability to accept God's ways and not question is imperative for the inner journey but, at the time, I didn't realize that. I didn't know that there was another dimension in which the old way of questioning became nonsensical and meaningless.

The emptiness was still there and it made me start wondering who or what was left to experience anything. If the old self had died then what was watching the inner happenings? All I knew was that something that was not me had broken into my sense of self, shattered it and *forced* me to experience my own nothingness. Upon closer inspection, I saw that it was the divine that brought my mind to a standstill and *this* was the beginning of the real transforming process. But this outside agency never gave itself away as the divine at the time this happened, so my initial experience of the divine was that of no-energy, no-self, no-will, no-nothing. This was my mind's original reaction to an infiltration by something outside itself.

A few weeks later, I had a dream about the inside of a building that had been completely cleaned out. The walls were the shiniest white I had ever seen and I took this to mean that my psychic dwelling had just been purged. A deeper center had opened and from now on my life would have to be lived without the former self.

Whenever a lesson was over, I always got something valuable from it, usually in the form of more insight into myself. But I never understood why God just didn't give up on me and pick on somebody else because, in my mind, I was a hopeless case. I turned my back on Him so many times that I was sure He would eventually desert me for good but He always waited till I calmed down and then sneaked in the back way. The puzzling aspect about this was that each time He returned, He made Himself at home a little closer than before. Seeing God's patience with my slow learning and how He never gave up on me made me love Him even more.

As I began to adjust to this state of interior nothingness, I saw that *this* was what's known as transforming union in mystical literature. A few years ago I believed that I was at an advanced stage in the process of transformation but now realized that the opening of the deeper center was just the *beginning* of the transforming process. The slow, eighteen-month decline to the bottom showed me my arrogant mistake.

The inner vacancy took on a different flavor when I resigned myself to living with it. I couldn't do anything about the void anyway and the blankness remained even during physical activity. The only thing to do now, I thought, was to let it be there for as long as it wanted.

It felt like an emptiness had smashed the ego and put *itself* in its place but the puzzling thing about this was that the emptiness seemed to be God Himself.

CHAPTER ELEVEN

EMPTINESS IS THE DIVINE

L iving without a sense of self wasn't the terrifying state I thought it was. It was very peaceful. There was no reaching out for anything because the driving desire *to* reach out was no longer there and even though old ways kept trying to kick life into themselves, they didn't get very far. The inner house was becoming quiet.

Every internal happening made me see that there really was a higher power who mapped out everything in advance just as a master architect would first design a building and then supervise all the construction. I couldn't imagine a superior intelligence leaving anything to chance and realized that whatever happens, inwardly and outwardly, was part of the great plan. It was a waste of time to try and change exterior situations because external events are only *reflections* of internal states. To change the outside, we have to first change the inside.

In retrospect, I saw that I never really controlled any results, external or internal, although my ego quickly took the credit for any positive changes that came along. With the realization that the ego wasn't a real entity, though, I understood that there's no one who could influence anything and it became obvious that what I called "my" life was nothing but a series of *impersonal events.* It was an unsettling surprise to see that all the nervousness and anxiety in the past was a big waste of energy because, in reality, there wasn't any me for "my" life to belong to.

Upon reflection, I realized that the course of events in everyone's life is premeditated by a higher intelligence and since individuality is an illusion, there's no one to gain the upper hand on anything. We're ultimately not responsible for making life move since we are not creators and can't create even the smallest thought. Whatever is, *must* be and if an event is preordained, there's nothing anyone could do to stop it from happening and if it's not, there's no individual on earth who can make it come forth. From then on, I understood more deeply than ever that I didn't have to push the river of life. *It flowed all by itself.*

Since it was all God's doing anyway, I learned to accept every situation that came along and lived with a calm indifference as to what transpired in my life. The self that worried about what might happen had disappeared and the old nature was no longer there to *feel* afraid. It was a relief to see that the things that used to scare me to death didn't have the impact they once did and a new fearlessness emerged. From that point on, my only desire was to experience *everything*, no longer wanting to timidly live *for* God but boldly *with* Him.

One afternoon I was riding my bicycle and noticed the hills in the distance covered with evergreens, saw their rolling contours against the sky, the tall pines a few feet from me and was conscious that there was no I looking at all this. I wondered who or what was making the body move because there was no "person" inside directing any of its maneuvers and I still wasn't able to put my finger on whatever it was that came to an end inside.

I kept asking myself, *"Exactly what was it that shut down?"*

What the Ego Is

From birth we have unconsciously taken ourselves for granted and because of this we can't imagine what it would be like to live without a sense of self.

When the sense of self shattered, I observed that no entity ceased to exist because there wasn't any real entity there in the first place, only a thought about being a separate individual, and I understood what the ego was only after the deeper center opened. It was deceptively obvious and I felt like someone who repeated a very dumb mistake all his life and never saw it for the blunder it was. I discovered that the ego is not an entity but an *activity*, a reflecting action of the mind, and that this can only be known in retrospect. It can't be seen for the error it is while living with it because the ordeal of a separate self has to *seem* like a real one, otherwise we don't get the full benefit of the experience.

In order to go through certain experiences, there had to be some driving energy pushing me to have them and it was obvious that this force had to be supplied from the *outside* because I couldn't manufacture it myself. This energy was behind the *feeling* of a personal self and I discovered that after the ego began to shut down, so did personal experiences. Events still happened but they no longer *felt* personal and it became increasingly evident that there can be personal experiences only when there's a personal *experiencer*.

It should be emphasized that *memories do **not** constitute a separate self* and in reality, there's no experiencer behind the experience, no seer behind the seeing, no talker behind the talking, and no thinker who does any thinking. It was clear that the body, along with its thoughts, feelings and habits was nothing but a programmed machine *without anyone in control* and that what others saw wasn't just what they got. What they saw was *all* they got.

A physical body in motion doesn't prove the existence of a person who's controlling it and I realized that the concept of a separate controller in each body is only a false assumption on our part. Upon closer observation, I saw that all my movements are nothing but unconscious transitions from one posture to another and that certain thoughts are *always* connected with specific positions.

They, too, are equally automatic and neither can be changed without affecting the other.

It became evident that if the body and mind influence each other then they must be of the same substance and continued reasoning in this direction brought me to the startling conclusion that if the organism is material then *everything* it produces must be material, *including the ego.*

For example, I watched my character change from one at home to a different one when driving and then to another one at work. The one that was present in the dentist's office last month was different from the one I had in the cookie aisle at the store this afternoon. The stunning aspect about this was that there was no director telling them to change and I concluded that the ego had to be a natural *function of matter.*

If personalities are energy, they are also tangible and can be *felt* and from that point on I understood the complete materiality of the human organism. Everything about it changes in response to a shift in external surroundings like the colors in a chameleon. I watched my personality change whenever there was a variation in external circumstances but there wasn't any conscious direction on my part. The changes were automatic responses to the external ambience.

CHAPTER TWELVE

God And I Are One

The period after hitting rock bottom brought a little relief. It consisted of the loosening of mental constrictions, the lifting of confusion and the gradual return of energy. But now there was a *new* feeling of life within and when dreams of a new dawn, a brand new land and a budding tree occurred, I knew the worst was over.

Feelings of an existence outside time increased in frequency but the immortality I felt clearly wasn't mine. It was an impersonal sensation of life that wasn't localized anywhere but seemed to be everywhere at once and the most impressive aspect was that it *knew* itself to be without end. It felt expansive, not restricted by space or time, and focusing on it produced a sensation of joy without reason. There was a feeling of fullness to it even though it didn't really contain anything except *itself*. The happiness of its own existence was its most striking feature.

Since this new life belonged to God and not me, I could only pinpoint it at my deepest center. It did not change my surface personality and nobody knew about it except Him and me. In fact, whenever I focused on it, there was the complete absence of any me at all.

I learned that life goes on the same way without a sense of self as it does with one and that things don't all of a sudden become rosy and problem free. Daily challenges still had to be met, groceries bought, bills paid and there were no outward indications to let others know that something had happened. This experience convinced me that God works in silence and doesn't need an audience to accomplish His goals.

A few days later, I was sitting in the living room and *felt* the words *spirit of God* within. As the feeling continued, I *knew* that this spirit was pure and innocent, like a crystal clear fire, and the more I concentrated on it, the stronger it became. It lasted all afternoon and in the early evening, this spirit revealed itself as the spirit of God.

I wrote the following in my notebook that day:

This is the day of realization that God's life and my life are the same—pure, untouched, unreachable, contained in nothing, containing everything. This spirit is Life itself.

The first realization of union with God occurred almost 30 years ago and I remember being surprised because being told that we are spirit and *actually experiencing it* are two different things. There were no qualities or attributes that I could point to and although I *knew* that God existed, I could not describe It. The ordinary mind can't relate an account of something that's beyond itself.

It's not that I knew *who* or *what* It is but *THAT* It is. There wasn't any who or what there and the only thing I could say with certainty is *THAT* It is and I *KNOW* that It is. This experience felt like a gigantic emptiness combined with a fullness that left no room for anything else and it let me know that God is everything but not a *personal* everything, just an *impersonal everythingness*. It was so quiet, so vast, so silently powerful that it felt like it was always worshiping itself, always giving itself the utmost homage.

Looking back on it, this realization was one of an interior union that had already been established in the unconscious and it was only after *unconsciously* living in this state that I understood that God and I are one. The recognition was new, the union wasn't. My interest in worldly things dropped sharply and the only thing that held my attention now was living with God or, more correctly, God living through me.

The startling quality of this perception eventually faded but the constant *feeling* that I am part of God and God is all of me remained. What surprised me, however, was that the initial impact of the experience did not last forever as I had imagined it would. The awareness settled into a very ordinary consciousness and although I knew about this experience, nobody on the outside did because no changes took place on the superficial level.

I've always been skeptical of Indian saints who say that they live in a constant state of ecstasy and bliss because statements like that never made sense to me. How long could you experience a constant state of *anything* before you got used to it? If you lived in a perpetual state of *any* feeling, you would eventually become accustomed to it and no longer notice it. It would become an ordinary and everyday experience.

In time, I saw that no insight or enlightenment lasted forever. They came and went. A perception that struck me as inspiring at one time would leave me feeling empty the next and I learned not to hold on to any experiences because they were just passing sensations and *not* an end in themselves. Every time they came, though, they felt like they would last forever.

Wanting to have mystical experiences repeated perpetuated the illusion that there was a me who can experience them again but it's the ego desiring something for itself, only now it wants something mystical instead of material. Clinging to higher experiences is just like holding on to anything else. The ego sets its sights on God so it can keep *itself* going. It's very cunning and the only reason it wants the divine is to keep the illusion of itself alive.

I've told God a number of times to stop sending mystical experiences because self-doubt always crept in when they ended and made me wonder if I did something wrong or offended Him somehow. I finally convinced myself that if God wanted me to have them, fine, but my personal preference was that they didn't come at all.

One Sunday I woke up and felt like I wanted to give energy to every living thing—trees, grass, insects, everything. During that afternoon, there was another strong perception that God and I are one but it was such a *natural* feeling that there was nothing *super*natural about knowing that we share the same life. Experiences like that only deepened my conviction that neither I nor anything else has a separate existence apart from the divine.

By that evening the experience had faded but it was such an expansive sensation that its temporary nature made it that much more attractive. Even after it ended, there remained this constant *feeling* of union with God. The only mental effort involved for making the connection with this sensation was disidentifying with thoughts.

Nothing comes in its full state all at once and I saw that God did not need to knock me over in order to impress me with His greatness, even though some of the experiences were so intense that I had to sit down and just let them happen. There were always mini-experiences of future states and I think it was these foretastes that were so copiously written about by the saints and mystics. The premonition of a higher state always seems like heaven when compared to the present one.

CHAPTER THIRTEEN

REALITY IS EVERYWHERE

E veryone makes a grave mistake in thinking that life becomes care free after the realization of Truth. It continues as usual but now there is an added dimension of consciousness and the *feeling* of being one with the divine. There is nothing supernatural about this state because we have to remember that God is our *natural* center, not the ego. When we reconnect with our natural core, we reconnect with God.

Spiritual reading no longer interested me because I felt that there was nothing more I could learn from books. The realization of It within was all that mattered and external spiritual activities lost their attraction. Everything on the outside was as nothing compared to His presence within and I realized that when the mind possesses God, it no longer needs to search for Him in externals.

The same went for spiritual exercises. Now that God was within, the practices were not necessary anymore and no matter how hard I tried to force an interest in them, I couldn't. All the studying and practicing was only a *preparation* to get me this far and now that the guest of honor was here, they were no longer needed. Even though my spiritual supports had brought me all the way to heaven's gate, I found that I could not bring any of them into the kingdom with me. I had to walk in empty handed.

It's spiritual law that everyone on the path has to build his own bridge to cross the river and this causeway consists primarily of paying attention to the unconscious and valuing Truth more than anything else in life. There are spiritual engineers all along the way giving helpful hints but we have to use our own material and our own efforts. The instructors can't build the bridge for us but can only provide us with the blueprints and offer encouragement.

I'd put a lot of time and energy into building my bridge and then found that I could not take it with me when I reached the other side. I wanted to but couldn't. Part of the problem was that spiritual practices had been such an integral feature of my life for so long that I could not imagine living without them and kept asking myself how anyone could *possibly* live a spiritual life without spiritual activities. But it was only my *identification* with these particulars that made me think that I couldn't get along without them.

Every time I picked up a spiritual book to read, a voice inside me said, *"No more books"* and was very insistent with its directive. This puzzled me a great deal because I couldn't tell whose side it was coming from. To abandon spiritual activities seemed very unspiritual but I discovered afterwards that it was necessary to give up what I *thought* constituted a spiritual life in order to have a *real* spiritual existence with God.

Every movement forward consists of leaving behind old supports to make room for new functions and when I could not force an interest in spiritual activities, I realized that this, too, was part of the plan. All the footholds along the way had to be dropped and nothing from the old life could be carried forward into the new. This includes attachment to spiritual books and disciplines.

It was time to live from the inside out and the only matter that held my interest now was the inner reality of the divine. I learned that sacrifice and inner study are necessary only up to a point but not forever, since the period for tuning and training is *before* the guest arrives, not after. We can't completely enjoy Its presence if we are engaged in some mental gymnastics, no matter how spiritual these activities seem to us. They are needed only during the unification process but once this inner congealing is complete, spiritual disciplines are no longer needed.

It seemed significant to me that self-study and renunciations produced no noticeable results when the inner journey changed its direction and I saw that once the unified state is reached, the inward movement comes to an end. It's finished. Its reversal no longer gave satisfaction in the secluded experience of mystical states, which I found added nothing to the enlightened condition, and my only thought was to go out and test its usefulness in the world.

Few people realize that the inward journey eventually changes course and becomes an *outward movement*. We can't go deeper than our deepest center and none of the former practices added one iota to the new state but it's not that I deliberately abandoned the tools that were helpful along the way. Rather, with the pearl of great price in hand, I discovered that any interest in further digging *automatically stopped*.

Looking back on it, I saw that everything I did in my spiritual journey was only a *mental activity* and had nothing to do with *real spirituality*, which is *not* a mental function at all. It consists of no thought, no identification, no self images, and nothing that can be *thought* about. If the mind can think about it, it's not spiritual.

I realized that the experience of God has nothing to do with the intellect and that Its presence is especially felt when there aren't any thoughts. Even though necessary mental exercises for slowing the mind, self remembering and self-observation are, in the long run, only preparations for another dimension of living and mental disciplines are valid only for a certain time. I eventually discovered that I didn't need a mind to know God any more than I needed a self to love Him.

It was a jolt to see that having an image of myself as a spiritual person was only a mental concept *about* myself. This caused quite a disturbance within because if my being spiritual was only a *thought about myself*, then was I really spiritual? The explanation is that true spirituality has nothing to do with *thoughts about* being spiritual. This is God's realm and extends beyond the mind and though the intellect can pose the question, it can never answer it. Only personal experience can do that. I had to let go of all self-identifications when God came, including my most cherished one of being spiritual.

Self-images are nothing but self-deceptions and eventually have to be given up. It's part of the inner dying process. Other than starting the search and gathering knowledge, the ordinary mind is not needed to experience God and this, I think, is the hardest of all for intellectuals. It means setting aside all their identifications with knowledge and for some people, useless knowledge of externals is all they have.

It was my strong identification with knowledge that provided the foundation for the illusion that there must be a person who possesses this knowledge but I eventually discovered that there can be no possessor of anything because, in reality, there is no separate self.

CHAPTER FOURTEEN

No Separate Self

I spent my whole life believing in myself and then found that I didn't exist the way I thought I did. Looking back, I saw that my belief in a separate self was two things at once. Firstly, it was a supposition of an individual me and secondly, a belief in other not-me's. The interaction with others enhanced the illusion of separateness but I discovered that a belief in my *self* presupposes a belief in other selves. One can't exist without the other and when the conviction of a separate me disappears, the notion of a separate you goes with it. When there's no me, there's also no you.

Since my certainty of an individual self was simultaneously an assumption in other isolated selves, it was a surprise to find that when one belief goes, so does the other. When I saw that there was no me on the inside, I also realized that there weren't any not-me's on the outside. There were only distinct physical appearances, bodies with habits, ideas, opinions, inclinations and desires but *no individuals.* Physical bodies existed but there were no "people" that they belonged to.

If we believe in something, we act as if it really exists and if we believe in the existence of a separate self, we are convinced that we have to protect and defend it. Our whole life will be spent defending something that *doesn't exist.* The good part is that once this notion is seen through, it can never be believed again. It's impossible to believe in something after we realize its falseness.

The idea of a separate self is the ultimate illusion, the cause of every personal misery, and centers around a me that imagines other not-me's doing bad things to it. *The suffering is real but the cause of it is illusory.* There are no selves "out there" doing anything to any self "in here" and realizing this is the beginning of spiritual maturity. It became evident that the notion of a segregated self was nothing but a *thought* that I mistook for an objective reality, something like being given a suggestion under hypnosis and then acting as if it were real.

Picture yourself standing inside a circle drawn on the ground. You've been hypnotized and told that you are unable to step outside that circle. You see people walking around and enjoying life but you never go beyond what you *believe* are your limits. From your standpoint, you feel isolated and left out.

What's the cause of your feeling of isolation? Seeing the other people enjoy themselves? No. It's your *unawareness* of your own invisible boundaries.

Nothing prevents you from stepping outside that circumference except your unconscious belief that you can't. Your thinking mind has been dulled and gullibly accepts a mental impression as an external reality. *You believe in imaginary limitations and **experience what you believe.***

We have been told from childhood that we're separate entities and over the years this notion crystallized into a hardened belief. Then we started *acting as if* we were distinct from everyone else and that's when all the trouble began. As adults, we found ourselves wishing we could step outside our present psychological limits but did not know how because we did not realize the nature of the problem.

Just as our physical bodies need a regular cleansing, so do our belief systems. Dropping old viewpoints and acquiring new ones turns life in a new direction that will be just as real to us as driving down a new highway.

One of the unworkable attitudes I left behind was the reliance on what others thought about me. Most of my life was spent allowing my feelings to be determined largely by what other people thought about me and it took years before I realized that it was *my* thought about *their* thought that caused the agonizing feelings. It was a big relief to see that when these damaging concepts stopped, so did the pain, and a soothing consolation to know that whatever could stop thought had to be stronger than it.

CHAPTER FIFTEEN

SEARCHING FOR GOD

My experiences told me that God is everywhere but there is a tendency to forget that everything invisible is also material. I used to have a hard time with the notion that spirit is matter but I think it's more truthful to say that matter is "objective" spirit and that this spirit is the *it* that everyone is looking for. Everyone thinks he should be looking for something invisible, so this conspicuous "objective" spirit is completely overlooked. People are searching all over for God when He's right there in their living room.

The paradox of it is that anyone who searches for Reality misses the obvious, which is that it's everywhere and closer to us than our own breath. When we look for this something, we look in different directions and miss the conspicuous fact that it's all around. Whoever searches for it discovers that there's nothing to find and then, like me, wonders what all the looking was about. Everyone disappears along the way and there ends up being no supreme being and no searcher, no prize and no contestant. All we have to do is *see* it but this seeing is both the easiest and hardest thing to do. It seems to be a *natural* function of the mind and introspection is the switch that turns it on.

In my opinion, everyone has to go through certain lessons regarding a separate self and like any other training course, *events have to come in a certain order.* We obviously can't experience the death of the ego before its development or the ordeal of giving it up before it has been completely experienced. This is why I firmly believe that the path to no ego has a predetermined course and that the inner stages we go through for union with the divine are the *same for everyone.* The circumstances that produce them are different but the experiential feelings are identical and occur in the same sequence.

It's also my firm conviction that the ego has its own life cycle. It is born, grows, and dies but in the larger context of the spiritual life, it's the *immature phase,* the juvenile stage before real maturity. It's when everything unconscious "in here" is projected "out there" and seen in the environment and other people, an everything-exists-for-me stage of living that is not seen for its immaturity until *after* it's passed through.

Although this phase is an immature one, it lays the immediate groundwork for the opening of a deeper center. It's an essential stage of the human experience and can't be avoided. We must remember that, in order to reach maturity, we have to first pass *through* immaturity. Spiritual adulthood lies on the other side.

Eventually I felt the utter ridiculousness of any kind of personal identification because, for me, it was sufficient to know that we were one with each other since we are one with God. It's my experience that we all have just *one* identity but if we believe we're separate, then we construct invisible walls between God and us. Seeing that individuality is an illusion gave me the understanding that separate entities exist only in the imagination and, in reality, there is no one to be a success or a failure, no one to be good or bad, and no one to be rewarded or condemned. My own sense of self was like a psychic barrier that prevented the experience of oneness with God and it became evident upon reflection that the way back to Him was to *unbelieve* this belief.

We have to return the way we came and realizing the imaginary nature of our personal existence is the only way to inner freedom.

CHAPTER SIXTEEN

INNER FREEDOM

S omething inside me knew that the emptiness was the beginning of inner freedom but my initial encounter with it was less than ecstatic.

It was so utterly different from anything I had known that my mind could not find a self-image to correspond to the new state and it panicked. But even though uncomfortable at first, it was strangely familiar. It felt like an immense vacuum inside, space without boundaries. Empty. Quiet. It was obvious that I had to travel spiritually on my own from now on because I could not follow someone else's teachings and be inwardly free at the same time.

In retrospect, I saw that the ego directed all its energy towards a certain goal and discovered that real freedom is the *absence* of any inner personal director. Such boundless liberty boggles the mind because there is no precedent for anything and *no entity inside wondering what to do*. Without the ego, there was no route for this energy to go because there was no one directing it anywhere.

The emptiness had a strange magnetic quality, as if it were pulling everything towards it, and I had to play a mental balancing act in order to maintain its quietness. Its silence contained a definite sense of another existence, one that was *complete*, and its peacefulness was easily accessible. Meditating on this stillness gave the feeling that it was something I'd wanted all my life.

A person won't go after something unless he first knows about it and I realized that most people don't seek this liberated state because they don't even suspect it exists. Imagine someone telling you that you just inherited a castle and that all you have to do is walk over and occupy it. You want to believe the informer but you have been lied to before and the information sounds so fantastic that you first want proof the castle exists. The problem is that you won't get this evidence until you take the initiative and see for *yourself*.

To be inwardly independent demands total surrender to something higher and I was initially terrified of giving up the illusion that I was in control of my life. I was scared that I would lose control over something I didn't have any control over to begin with but in the end, I found that I didn't give up anything at all. I merely surrendered the *illusion* that there was someone surrendering.

The only agency that can change anyone is God and I saw that inner liberty belonged to Him and Him alone. No human being can claim it exclusively as his own personal possession or give it to anyone else. It's an inner realization and *not* something that can be transmitted but I think there are special conditions that can induce it. These conditions revolve around the practice of mental stillness and seem to be more an expression of the state rather than necessary qualifications.

Inner freedom is liberty from the known self and there is a sense of vastness inconceivable to the everyday mind but we seem to have a problem here. If this state is beyond the ordinary mind then how can anyone attain it? I believe the answer is that the self that is asking the question *can't* attain it because in order to experience it, this self has to disappear. The state of nonexistence that terrified me so much turned out to be the inner liberty I always wanted but I had to first stop being *me*. It was obvious that I couldn't hold on to my old identity and be inwardly free at the same time.

An illustration can help understand this.

Picture a man standing inside a walled enclosure. He was raised within those walls and thought that the only life that existed was the one he was familiar with. A few people told him about another world but he didn't believe them.

After a while, a strange uneasiness set in. He yearned for a life outside the walls but didn't know anything about it, so he read what others had to say. Eventually he wanted it more than anything else in the world.

One day an explosion shattered a small opening in one of the walls and exposed another world beyond his enclosure. The sight of the unfamiliar made him freeze in terror but in time, he relaxed and saw that the outside life wasn't frightening at all. By his own efforts, he made a bigger opening in the wall so he could step outside and as soon as he did, the walls began to dissolve. He saw that he was free and always was. The walls that seemed so real existed *only in his imagination.*

That's what inner freedom is like. When we are surrounded by imaginary walls all our lives and then suddenly faced with the experience of no walls, it stuns the mind. Inner liberty is the experience of life with no self labels, no personal boundaries, and no mental images.

If you are nobody in the eyes of the world and no one in particular to yourself, then you are everything Truth wants you to be. Wanting to see your *resistance* to being free sends a powerful prayer to heaven and lets God know that you are ready for a change in your inner nature.

He does the rest and eventually brings you to the unified state.

CHAPTER SEVENTEEN

THE UNIFIED STATE

We have to understand that the realization of Truth doesn't obliterate our humanity. It *completes* it. The path to it, though, is not an additive process as most people believe but rather a shedding one. *It's a progressive death to everything that makes up the personal self.* Once beyond this point, being holy or wicked is no longer possible because there's no one left to be either one.

After the deeper center opened, I learned to accept every feeling that came along and not question or resist it. Since God is all there is, I saw that all my thoughts and feelings were *His*, not mine, and that I ultimately wasn't responsible for any violent or gloomy ones. The old way of resisting now seemed unsuitable. God is completeness and every act and feeling is His.

With this realization, I understood that whatever we experience is all right because it belongs to God, not us, and that there was nothing personal in any feeling. It was quite a surprise to experience an emotion without thinking that it was mine. Feelings presented themselves as impersonal forces and I saw that they don't belong *to* us because they don't come *from* us. There is nothing personal about anything we think, feel or do because we are incapable of originating any thought, feeling or action. Everything belongs to God.

Since my life was no longer mine but belonged to Him, I felt that I didn't have any business asking questions like *"Why is this happening?"* or *"Why am I doing this?"* It was no longer *my* life. The question seemed inappropriate and senseless because there wasn't any *me* doing anything anymore, just an impersonal power acting through this body.

My experiences told me that the unified state is primarily a *we* consciousness, God and I, and that at our deepest level of being we are one with the divine. All along the way, though, there were realizations that It is all there is and permeates all matter and even though there are different physical contours, no object has a separate existence of its own. This applies not only to inanimate things but to human beings as well. Human bodies have different shapes but not one of them has its own existence or even the existence of a separate entity that occupies it.

The realization of the divine is actually part of the *total human experience* and can be achieved by anyone with sufficient dedication. Since the ego cannot shut itself off and knows nothing about opening a deeper center, I saw that this state can be reached only after submitting to the experience of spiritual death. Since transformation is an inner growth process, events have to occur in a certain sequence and according to their own schedule. There wasn't anything I could do to hasten things and I learned that letting the process happen *without resistance* was the hardest part of all.

Somewhere in the back of my mind, however, was the creeping illusion that union with God meant to be a little bit more divine than human. I kept waiting for this to happen and couldn't understand why it didn't but that it never occurred apparently is not what the mystical life is about. The expectation for God to make me divine was a failure on my part to fully accept my *completely human* nature. My notion of perfection was self-centered and the reality of the situation went against all my speculations of what completion is. We don't become more divine than human but rather experience another dimension *in addition* to our humanity. Now we are human with God.

Upon realizing that human nature is complete *in itself*, I saw that I could never go against myself because there was no more inner division. The sense of knowing its completeness was satisfying in itself and all the intensity was in its depth of feeling. I discovered that the surface mind wasn't needed most of the time and it especially wasn't needed to *know* that God exists. Something deeper had opened and was more on the level of being and I found myself becoming more annoyed each day with the chattering in my mind.

At this stage, I realized that no matter what I did, felt or thought, I can never go against my own nature and saw that *this* was the meaning of the unified state. Accepting *everything* as part of us is the end of inner division and, in reality, we cannot contradict ourselves because nothing can go against its own essence. When we see our own *completely human* nature, we also realize the character of every other person on earth. Knowing this feels sufficient in itself and there is no longer a desire to be anything other than what we already are.

In order to realize this, though, illusions about being anything than basically human have to be punctured. When we are completely human, we are on the same level as everyone else and there's no superior or inferior, only a feeling of completeness and fullness. We can only think human thoughts, feel human feelings, and do human things. We can't have any experiences other than human ones.

It's a great disservice to God and humanity for mystical authors to tell us that the unified state is reserved for only a privileged few. It's the *natural* goal of every human being and, in my experience, one realized rather quickly when the dedication is sufficient. Our job is to understand that the realization of Truth is possible while *still on earth* instead of believing that it exists only in the future. There is no future in eternity.

I discovered that, in the unified state, there is no such thing as *my* true self as opposed to *your* true self. There is only *one* real self and the experience of union with God is the same for all. With this realization, I saw that my whole life was spent trying to transform a self that not only was incapable of being transformed but *didn't exist to begin with.*

Everyone makes a grave mistake by thinking he has a self that's capable of being changed into something else. The truth is that there's nothing that transforms because the ego is *not* an entity and something that doesn't exist can't mutate into something divine. The years that I spent changing my attitudes and practicing new behavior probably helped my character but that's about it. My belief that I was transforming a sinful self was a gigantic hoax *and the joke was on me.*

The trouble with the concept of inner transformation is that it forever clings to the notion that there is a self that is capable of being transformed. There isn't. The self is only a *mental activity* and the paradox of inner transformation is that we are saved when we realize that there is no one there *to be* saved.

The sooner we let go of the belief that we have a self that needs to be transformed, the sooner we will experience our real spiritual identity. I think that a sincere desire to have this happen has a lot to do with it but in the long run, all desires come from God. When the time comes for us to realize that His life and our life are the *same*, He puts the desire in us to start looking for Him.

It's not that we first have the desire for this and then God fulfills it. I think it's the other way around. He gives the soul the desires *He* intends to accomplish in it because left all to ourselves, we would not know what to ask for. This was the only way I could account for the even match between my desire to find God and its eventual reality.

I've often wondered whether reincarnation exists or not and eventually saw that the subject can only be settled by inner gnosis. My experiences told me that it exists up to a certain level and then doesn't hold true anymore because once the entity that needed to come back dissolves, the question of who or what reincarnates becomes a nonsensical issue.

When I saw that the ego didn't truly exist, I also understood that, ultimately, *there is nothing that reincarnates*. With the realization of It within, a physical body remains but there is no longer an entity, so reincarnation exists and doesn't exist simultaneously. It's true only as long as something remains that needs to be lived through but when this something disappears, there is nothing left to come back. Reincarnation is valid only for a certain time but *not forever*.

CHAPTER EIGHTEEN

UNIFICATION OF SPIRIT AND MATTER

With the realization that everything is material, I saw that the division between spirit and matter was only a mental concept and ultimately false. *Everything* for me became a spiritual activity and every happening was holy because it was done by God. Heaven was right here on earth and I was in church all the time.

The imaginary separation between the earthly and the spiritual applied not only to activities but to objects as well. To distinguish between the two is to impose an illusory boundary on God, call one part spiritual and the other earthly, and then judgmentally proclaim one better than the other. But when seen from a unified perspective, *there is no such thing as a spiritual activity apart from an earthly one.*

It was no longer a matter of either spiritual reading or doing the dishes because I found that the most mundane action, when done with the awareness of God, becomes a prayer. Putting away the groceries was a moving meditation and I saw that it was the division in *us* that divides life into the material and spiritual. When the inner split disappears, so does the outer one.

Everything for me converged into oneness and although I saw the outline of physical objects, something inside *felt* the unity of everything. My physical eyes saw the exterior shapes of things but the boundaries that separated them no longer existed. Underneath I experienced unity.

I don't believe that there is such a thing as a spiritual life apart from a material one because spirit and matter are the *same*, not irreconcilable opposites. The most spiritual life we could ever have is an earthly one in which God is no longer seen as an external entity but experienced as an *internal reality*. When we walk with God, every place we go is sacred.

At this time, I saw that there were some wolves who were tending the sheep and telling them that it's easier to find Truth in one of the sacred hot spots of the earth. I don't believe that any geographical place is better than another for spiritual growth and we don't have to go anywhere to experience Truth. No physical locality can "do" anything for us because only God can perform the inner change and He doesn't need us to be anywhere except right where we are. Growth proceeds from the inner to the outer, *not* the other way around.

This can be illustrated with a story.

The Secret Monastery

Once upon a time there was a man who traveled all over the world looking for Truth but didn't find it anywhere.

One day a friend told him that Truth could be found in a secret monastery far away. He said that the monastery wasn't easy to reach and that it took along time to get to and that only one monk who found Truth lived there. The news made the man very excited. The whole story about a secret monastery seemed shrouded in thrilling mystery.

"If only one wise monk lives there," he thought, *"then he can surely tell me how to find Truth."*

And he set off on his journey.

The way to the monastery was rougher than he thought. The streets were narrow and the people who promised to help him were unreliable. A group of men who said they would carry his luggage for him turned out to be robbers who stole the suitcases along with his money. The local guides who said that they alone knew the way through the dense forest turned out to be so superstitious that they ran when a sudden storm occurred, shouting that the spirits were warning them to turn back. The man had to travel all alone.

One difficulty after another arose and after awhile he grew very weary.

"It's just not worth it," he thought. "Maybe the monastery doesn't really exist. Or maybe the whole thing was just made up." He sank into deep despair.

He stopped on a hillside to rest and thought about how gullible he was to believe such a story. After a few minutes he spotted a solitary building behind some trees and something in him knew that he had found his monastery. He ran toward it.

He reached the door catching his breath and knocked. It opened right away as if someone were standing behind it and what the man saw surprised him. He expected to see a bearded monk wearing a long robe but instead saw a short, clean shaven man wearing a wrinkled shirt and baggy pants.

"What do you want?" the man said in a very matter-of-fact voice.

The visitor was dumbstruck because he wasn't sure whether this was the monk and wondered whether this was the monastery.

"If this is a monastery then I'm looking for the monk who lives here," he said.

"That's me," said the short man. "How can I help you?"

The visitor had a hard time believing this. Finally he said, "I've traveled all over the world looking for Truth and heard that It could be found here and I've come to find It."

Without missing a beat the monk said, "When you were traveling all over the world looking for Truth, did you find It anywhere?"

"No, I didn't," replied the visitor.

"Then you won't find it here either," the monk said.

You don't have to go to holy mountains or sacred places to find Truth. Even if you have never been inside a church in your life, it's still possible to experience union with the divine *here and now*. But you have to make the first move. The realization of the divine within gives real inner strength because it's no longer an outside power but an internal reality and searching on the outside disappears. But as long as you think of God only as an external deity, you will never experience Its subjective reality within. In order to experience the inner divinity, all your present concepts and ideas about God as an external power or a supernatural being have to go. You can't hold on to the belief that God exists outside of you and experience Its presence within at the same time.

I think that the divine can best be understood as our *natural* center with a specific, creative energy all its own and only a life lived from this center is worth living. It's my opinion that a life lived entirely from the ego is remarkably dull not only for the person himself but for all concerned. Living completely requires more than just a stale ego. It needs spirit because this alone is capable of giving vital expression to those spiritual potentialities that lie beyond the reach of the personal self.

I discovered that the inner kingdom is not a state of all positives and no negatives like most people believe. It's a state of *no* opposites, no two-ness and no one-ness either. That Reality is not two means that it has no dividing lines. It's life without opposites and therefore without the imaginary boundaries that created them.

Since the mind can only think in terms of twoness, it can't conceive of existence as a singularity. If it does, it immediately divides it into two parts, calling one part me and one part you, past and future, inner and outer. These divisions exist only in the mind but not in reality. Duality consists of an *inseparable* twoness and either exists in its binary form or doesn't exist at all, so if one side disappears, the other goes with it. In other words, if the sense of me disappears, so does the sense of you because the illusion of a separate me created the idea of an individual you. In order to experience all of life, it's necessary not to call any action good or bad, any feeling pleasurable or painful, since it's the labeling of things into their apparent opposites that causes problems. Living completely means existing without the division between me and you, good and bad, pleasant and unpleasant.

When you label your emotional states, you manufacture imaginary boundaries around them and then try to avoid the bad ones. But you're not allowing yourself to experience the wholeness of life by avoiding any feelings. God, Truth, Reality is life without opposites, experience without labels, and existence without identifications. When there are no mental boundaries, there is no you and this state of no you is what you have always wanted.

One time I was in a grocery store and felt uncomfortable and resisted the feeling because it was an unpleasant sensation. At first I didn't want to look at it and then realized that being comfortable and uncomfortable are two parts of *one feeling* and that neither one can be gotten rid of, so I kept both sides in consciousness at the same time. Surprisingly, the unpleasant sensation went away.

To divide the feelings into pleasant and unpleasant parts is to superimpose an imaginary boundary on a whole sensation and then only want to experience half of it. This can't be done. Since we contain totality within us, we are going to experience all of life whether we like it or not and resistance to this totality makes us divide life into the good and bad.

Feelings don't have real boundaries and I discovered that experiencing both sides *at the same time* is what transforms them. Something of a miracle occurs and the two opposing sensations combine and form a new resultant that gives a definite impression of completeness. Try it for yourself and see. It may feel uncomfortable at first but give it a chance to do its good work. It helps to remember that in order to experience something *new*, you have to try something *different*.

I used to have a recurring dream that said that *everything* on the way to enlightenment must be experienced and it emphasized the word everything. I took this to mean that something catastrophic was about to occur but later understood that it was saying that both sides of a feeling or situation must be experienced *at the same time*. Experiencing everything *at once* was its message, including the feelings we've been avoiding.

All feelings are part of the human experience and you have to experience all of them in order to realize your complete nature. Consciously experiencing both at the same time is the important thing, so it doesn't matter which contradictory sensations you experience. When you accept *everything* about yourself, you will never be at issue with anything you do because there won't be any inner division, no one part against another part.

This is the unification process. If you do it to one set of impressions, you do it to all of them because it is the *doing* that's important, not which feelings are used.

The experience of completeness comes afterwards and there can never be contradiction whenever both sides are felt simultaneously. Feelings and desires are no longer experienced partially but completely. Inner conflict ends. Life will take on an added dimension because you are allowing yourself to *feel* more. Being complete means living completely and avoiding nothing. God is all emotions and when you feel both sides of a feeling *at the same time*, you are very close to the kingdom.

Imagine yourself sitting in your living room looking out the window. It looks gloomy outside and not much light is coming through the glass. You get up to see what the weather is like and notice that the sun is shining but it still appears dark inside. Approaching the window lets you see that the glass is dirty, so you take a rag and wipe it. The cleaner it gets, the more light comes in. Finally, your whole living room is filled with sunshine.

Wanting to experience only half of a situation is like looking through a window that's spotted with dirt. You let in only some of the light but the problem is not a lack of sunshine. It's the murky glass. Walking to the window symbolizes your personal effort to find out why you don't have more light and wiping the glass is your attempt to experience the whole of a feeling. The more you clean the window, the more sunlight you have in your living room.

During a particularly trying period, I saw that I caused my own discouragement by expecting things to turn out a certain way. When they didn't, it felt like I was on an emotional roller coaster going from high expectation to deep despair. Then I realized that expectation and despair are two parts of the *same feeling* and held both sensations in consciousness at the same time, feeling the whole emotion instead of just part of it. At first, it felt like I'd go crazy but experiencing both simultaneously gave a sensation of completeness afterwards.

All feelings are complete in themselves and it is only our false perception that divides them and calls one part easy, the other hard. They are all part of the journey home and none can be eliminated but the imaginary boundaries that we impose on them can. When we don't divide a sensation, both sides are felt without resisting its opposite.

That's when I realized that completeness is purity, something that has no division and is therefore whole. An impure sensation is contaminated with imaginary sections but a pure one is not. I saw that spirit, which is pure because it is untouched by the mind, is *without any imaginary division*. When opposite feelings toward a situation or person are consciously experienced at the same time, we are living a *whole and complete life*.

Purity has nothing to do with sin but is an experience of wholeness that transcends the mind. It is uncontaminated by mental division and the strange thing about it is that purity can be *felt*. It is a feeling of completeness combined with an inner knowing that it is beyond the reach of any thought.

It's the sensation of having life more abundantly.

CHAPTER NINETEEN

To Have Life More Abundantly

One night I had a dream about a map of the south-eastern U.S. in which all the states were outlined in red, with Florida being conspicuously the lowest state. About a month later, I experienced intermittent desires to live and to die and these gradually increased in intensity until it felt like I was being internally ripped apart. Since Florida is our "lowest" state, I understood that my unconscious was telling me that the deepest state of my inner country had been reached.

A few weeks later, the desires to live and die occurred so rapidly and forcefully in succession that I saw they weren't coming from me but belonged to something primordial. After being thrown back and forth by them for a while, I eventually realized that they were *two sides of one living force* and are the energies that keep everything in a constant state of transformation. These urges, as far as I could tell, surface only upon reaching the deepest level of being.

This primordial power contained within itself both the urge for existence and extinction *at the same time,* two opposing desires of a unified whole. It used to appear periodically in my dreams and had a numinous quality about it, taking the forms of the most heterogeneous figures, some masculine, some feminine, and sometimes

115

alternating between the two. I understood that the meaning of these symbols was contained in themselves, not in
any personal experiences, and that their qualities were so
interchangeable that they weren't concretely either male or
female.

Shortly after, these diametrical energies turned into the
experience of life with a capital L and I knew that the most
deep seated state of existence had been reached. Neither
force canceled the other and their unification felt like a
state of *completion* rather than one of ultimate craziness. I
understood that life, at its deepest level, is the desire to
exist and not exist *at the same time* and the conscious experience of their fusion is what Christ referred to when He
said to have life more abundantly.

This primordial force is not an entity but an impersonal,
creative power that has always existed and is *not* a being,
although it created all the gods and the whole universe
gets its life from this force. I was given the insight that all
the forms it animates are two dimensional and have no
real existence of their own. It gives life to forms and then,
after a while, withdraws it *back into itself* for renewal.
Always in the process of creating, it not only was the giver
and taker of animation but the only life there is. Nothing
else *really* exists.

This experience of increased vitality was not under my
conscious control and it didn't transform me into a
dynamo but had a different sensation from energy, a
distinct feeling all its own. I could not give it to anyone or
use it for anything and didn't need to think about it for it
to be there because it originated beyond the mind. Everyday life went on just as before. It didn't interfere with any
surface functions but was felt deep in the center of my
being and it let me know that real life has nothing to do
with anything that anyone could *think* about. The only
thing that can be said about this force is that it *exists*.

After experiencing absolute emptiness, I realized that
extinction is what terrifies everyone the most and that all
our activities are frantically meager attempts to keep us
from facing the reality of our individual non-existence. It's

our fearful resistance to nonexistence that prevents us from experiencing true life but, rightly understood, the death of the ego is our only salvation. It's a grave mistake to think that we can contact God while still believing in our separate existence because in order to reach the deepest level of life, the personal self has to first die. Most people don't realize that if they don't go through the death of the personal self, they will only have what they *call* life, which will be their imagined separate existence, but they will never know *true* life.

Since there is nothing personal about this force, there was no sense of me in this dimension, no entity who could say "*I* am this." God doesn't know Itself the way we know ourselves and it's human presumption to think that It has a self the way we have one. We believe that we are separate masters in our own house only because we like to flatter ourselves but in reality, nothing exists but God.

The illusion of being a separate individual is the biggest bluff of all but once we see that only God exists, we *become* one with this creative power. From then on, my smallest action became just as important as any other and I discovered that any work performed with the awareness of the divine felt sacred. The most menial task had a feeling of satisfaction to it and I didn't feel that anything was beneath me to do. In my mind, there was no distinction between a corporate executive and a janitor because the difference between them disappears when experienced with God.

Since we are not the givers of life, I saw that our pleas not to have it taken away carry no weight and that everyone misses the mark by thinking that individual souls are immortal. It's important to remember that *anything* with a beginning will also have an end and that the mightiest superpowers will return to oblivion but this impersonal energy will continue creating. The whole process of transformation, as I saw it, was the descent, or ascent, into deeper levels of being and eventually we hit the innermost dimension of life. This sensation of inner fullness is the *treasure hard to attain* which, I believe, pushes itself to the surface after sufficient time is put into brooding introspection.

I arrogantly assumed that the worst was over when I reached the deepest part of my being and didn't know that the most frightening encounter was about to take place. Not only does abundant life reside at our deepest center but so does our most deep seated fear and we activate this sleeping dragon when we get to the bottom of our being. In order to arrive at the pearl of great price, this demon has to be experienced and lived through and I saw that God didn't make an exception in my case.

Our deepest fear is always associated with the loss of whatever we are identified with the most and for me, it was running out of money. This fear can only be overcome by facing it and life put me in exactly those circumstances where it seemed imminent. Later I understood that *fear is only a thought* but because I didn't see this, I found something external to be afraid of.

I quit a good job to devote my time to Truth and eventually had to have an income again but life saw to it that I didn't get it. No matter how hard I tried to find work or establish an income, nothing happened. I was constantly thrown back on myself so that I could experience what I was really like underneath and it was emotionally uncomfortable. I discovered that a change in attitude didn't alter the external situation and my mind desperately raced around trying to find an image to fit the circumstances but it could not.

I found myself not wanting to confront this terror and wishing that I'd never started the inner journey in the first place but life put me in the precise situation where I had to face it. I fiercely resisted it at first and then figured that if it was in God's plan, so be it. Upon accepting this fear as part of me, its reign of terror ended and a sort of miracle occurred because I no longer considered having no money and no apartment a big deal anymore.

When first coming upon this deep seated threat, I didn't see it as part of me and didn't know that I was fighting *myself* but after accepting it into my life, I ended up feeling good about something that used to scare me to death. Paradoxically, I felt more *complete.* What was once my biggest fear and most important issue turned into something that didn't terrify me anymore. Eventually I saw that thought was the cause of fear and that without fearful thoughts, there was no fear.

Afterwards I realized that all our activities are nothing but desperate attempts to avoid facing our own nothingness and that underneath all the running around, the relationships, jobs, traveling and TV is a disturbing emptiness. This is what scares everyone the most, *not* external circumstances, and I saw that anxious feelings about it didn't have a leg to stand on without fidgety thoughts to back them up.

This experience told me that the journey home is one of coming to terms with all our inner devils and it was only in retrospect that I understood this to be the final descent into hell which, in my case, lasted nearly five months. It was a painful cleansing process, and a necessary one, since we can't have any unconscious fear and experience God's courage at the same time. In order to make it to the sixth grade, we have to go *through* all the lessons of the fifth. No skipping grades allowed en route to the True Self.

CHAPTER TWENTY

THE TRUE SELF

My own inner journey showed me that the ego filters all experiences through itself and thus sees everything as *it* is. If we mix this in with the mind's natural function to divide everything, we end up with an enormous capacity for self-delusion, the imaginary many created from the un-dividable one. Not only is "out there" fragmented into separate objects but every other human body is seen as a separate entity, either friend or enemy, someone to be avoided or an object to be pursued.

Just as the ego experienced the divine through *itself* and described this feeling as I, so does the deeper self experience the divine through *itself* and calls the feeling I. The true self is *not* the divine but the spectrum of consciousness that experiences the divine much more intensely than the ego did.

I discovered that, although God is experienced *through* the true self, it doesn't mean that the individual has become divine. Carl Jung in *Symbols of Transformation* wrote that *"...the experience of God within is a real but purely subjective phenomenon and that God is the name man gives to this powerful feeling..."* When coming upon this state, I realized that it was the experience of a powerful internal reality, *not* an external deity, and that every feeling that filters into consciousness calls itself I, including this intense

sensation of life and being. It was strong enough to obliterate every thought except the one that says, *"I am God."*

The true self can't be given to anyone because it's a
shedding process of everything that belongs to the personal
self—but keep in mind that even though it's called a self,
the true "self" is *not* an entity. It's what's left *after* the sense
of personal self is gone, which is why we can't think ourselves into this realization. This range of consciousness is
so permeable that it allows the experience of the divine to
filter through more easily than at lower levels—and experience is the only way to know that we exist with God.

Nothing can be truly understood until it has first been
lived and we can't get the assurance of eternal life by
thinking about it. This state is an experiential growth into
spiritual maturity and can't be hastened any more than we
can speed up the process of maturity by teaching it. Its
development needs a long period of incubation and all we
can do is talk about our own experiences and share them
with others.

The first realization of this spiritual identity was
startling because it was an encounter with something
outside the mind and I could not adequately describe the
true self when it was experienced. The everyday mind can
only relate to things that exist on its own mental level and
falls silent if it comes upon anything it doesn't recognize. If
we use the intellect to shape our understanding of God, we
will wrongly conclude that we "know" Him.

Afterwards, the startling revelation gave way to a very
unspectacular state of awareness and I saw that *this* was
the original state of purity and innocence in which God
intended all men to live. It was this encounter that told me
that we are all going in the same direction, all drawn by
the same force and ultimately come to the same end—
union with God.

We're shortchanging ourselves if we think that the
mystical life is nothing but a full-time, flowery experience.
It's not about a continuous state of rapture and bliss but
about putting Truth first in our life. It's about living without the division between an inner and outer, you and me,

good and bad. It's about knowing that God is in every thing because every thing is *in God*.

It's my experience that the divine is a subjective fact of human life, otherwise there would never be any talk of the divine, and I think that mystical authors perform a great injustice if they say that this state is reserved for only a chosen few. If we go beyond their highly emotional descriptions of their first encounters with it and take a realistic look at the state, it turns out to be a very ordinary and un-supernatural consciousness. *This is the* **natural** *state in which God intended every person to live.* There's nothing supernatural about *that.*

Even though the divine experience had surfaced, I recognized that it was not mine and that no human being can claim it as a personal possession. This reinforced my belief that life uses us as an expression of *Itself* and I realized more profoundly than ever that what I called *my* life was really none of my business.

It belongs to God.

CHAPTER TWENTY-ONE

SEARCH FOR TRUTH

I t's important to remember that whoever searches for Truth is *transformed* in the process. No one ever remained the same at the end as he was in the beginning because looking for Truth guarantees the dissolution of the person doing the looking. The individual who ends up knowing Truth is *not* the same one who started the search.

Truth wants to take what is unreal from us and give us something genuine in exchange but in our state of waking sleep, we think that it's trying to take something valuable. Suppose you had a $15 bill in your pocket and believed that it was real money. Not realizing it was counterfeit, you'd mistrust anyone asking you to exchange your phony currency for a genuine $10 bill. Similarly, Truth is attempting to get us to give up our unreal life, which we assume is real, for the genuine article.

My own experience showed that the beginning part of the journey is intellectual and empowered by a deeper urge to notice inner opposites. At this phase, the mind *believes* that there's a searcher and something to be found but in the end, there's no prize and no contestant either. Only an inner stillness remains that gets more profound after the mind gets used to the shocking realization that there's *no one* inside.

Inner reality cannot be seen by the masses but can be *experienced* by individuals but the trouble is that it's so well hidden that everyone misses it. If the mind searches, there's movement by the mind and it's lost, like trying to recover a coin at the bottom of a pool. The more you splash around looking for it, the harder it is to see, which is why no one can intellectually think themselves into this state. This condition is disassociated from everything and completely untouched by the mind. When coming upon this state, I saw that the divine is not only non-dual, It's also non-One because there's no one left who can say *"I am God."* There is just an impersonal *everythingness* that is a law unto itself.

So if it's not a supreme being but it's everywhere and it's *real*, how do you describe it? Now I know why mystical literature has so little to say on the subject. Even if I wrote for the next hundred years, I couldn't possibly convince anyone of its reality even though its existence is so obvious to me.

The paradox is that it's everywhere yet cannot be given to anyone or used for anything and one of the disappointing surprises for me was that I found there was no way to share it with others or even assure them of its existence. It was like standing in the middle of an ocean without being able to give the water to anyone. This is probably a safeguard because if someone found he could give it away, he would consider himself God and this would be equivalent to satanic conceit. Given human nature, it would only be a small step away from selling it.

I think more people than we are led to believe have reached this stage but did not leave any written records behind and if they did, they weren't published. This is not a state that goes around jubilantly pointing to itself but is content to stay in the background and doesn't need anyone's attention. It's satisfied to just *be there*, completely unnoticed.

Just as there's a channeling craze going on now with people channeling everyone from intergalactic entities to the Absolute, I predict there will be an enlightenment craze occurring in the next ten years. People will go around saying, *"I found it, I found it,"* but if anyone who says that he found it also claims that he can help *you* find it, hold on to your wallet. That's pure ego talking. Nobody can help anyone find God because only God can do that and eventually all such outside "help" must be given up. The person has to see that it's an *individual* search. There are no couples in heaven and no one can enter the kingdom holding somebody else's hand. Everyone has to walk in single file.

There is a temptation for me now to suggest that no one search but this would not satisfy the earnest seeker. I never liked hearing that myself. Wanting to know a deeper Reality is like an irritating itch that won't leave you alone and when you ask others what to do about it, they say, *"Don't scratch it."* Not scratching it doesn't make it go away and doesn't alleviate its nagging irritation.

So what do I tell others? Not to search? Nobody wants to hear that because then they would have to give up the self-image of being a spiritual seeker and that, for me at least, was my most cherished identity. What a shock to find out that I could not bring any personal concepts into heaven, no matter how spiritual they seemed to me.

The fact that Reality is everywhere and I missed it for so long is what I find so amazing but what surprises me even more is how few know that such a state exists. Some people probably have never heard that the *inner experience* of God is possible and those who do sense that they're searching for *something* but aren't sure for what.

Truth is like a secret treasure buried so deep that it can only be found by persistently digging for it and the hardest part is to keep shoveling even after all your friends have completely abandoned you. This world discourages introspection and I now see why it's so important to be around others who also want to find it. If you don't, you can easily lose sight of your aim.

Time and again, I saw that a higher power controlled all internal changes that occurred, regardless of whether I agreed with these changes or not, and that dreams altered

my attitudes and viewpoints without any conscious partic-
ipation on my part. Continued observation revealed that if
the so-called unconscious is in control of adjusting the conscious standpoint, then maybe it's not so unconscious after
all but a kind of higher consciousness that knows what it's
doing and does it without regard for any personal feelings
about the matter. Eventually I understood that what we
call the unconscious only *seems* non-conscious from our
limited perspective but is actually a spiritual *super*conscious.

Experience brought to light that this superconscious is
spirit and although it *feels* like an independent being, is
actually the third person of the Trinity, the spirit of God.
Spirit controls our inner destiny, adjusts our conscious
attitudes through dreams and *it* does all the inner work of
transformation, *not us*. It's pure imagination to think that
we have a self capable of transforming itself because an
imaginary entity can't produce any authentic changes.
Only something real can perform genuine alchemy and
this real something is Truth.

I firmly believe that God takes twice as many giant steps
towards us for each small one we take in His direction but
we don't know this at first since we are walking in the
dead of night. I think traveling in darkness is a necessary
stage, otherwise we would egotistically believe that we can
make it on our own and save ourselves but we can't. If we
raise a finger, it's God doing it, if we think a thought, it's
God doing it, and if we live at all, it's because of Him. So if
we can't even *exist* on our own, how can we possibly *make*
it on our own?

One of the things I never liked was that, all along the
way, no one would tell me how long it took or even if
finding Truth was guaranteed. I think most people don't
know the length of time and I also think that those who do
know deliberately withhold it from those asking. It's a
device to keep the seeker from giving up. In my case, it
took almost ten years *once the dedication was sufficient* and
making the persistent efforts to get *that* far was the hardest
part. But after devoting every ounce of my being to Truth,

I found that there was swift progress made, especially in the later stages.

And these stages are timeless.

CHAPTER TWENTY-TWO

ETERNITY IS TIME-LESS

M ost people have trouble with the word eternity. They imagine it to be a very, very long time and something that lasts forever but the mystic doesn't understand eternity that way at all. Eternity is not an awareness of everlasting time but an awareness *without* time and nothing obscures the divine light so completely than the contamination of time. It's one of the major obstacles between God and us.

I personally feel that the notion of everlasting time is a monstrosity and impossible to mentally conceive. All feelings of guilt are linked to the past and all anxiety is tied to thoughts of the future, so to live in time is to live in mental torment. This is *not* how Truth intended us to live.

We can think about time since it's a mental creation but we can also experience an existence outside of it. The true self lets us plunge into eternity and experience the unborn and undying, life *outside* of time, but the reason we feel that the present moment is pressed between the past and future is that we have imposed a false boundary upon the timeless present. We fragmented eternity into the opposites of past and future and then conceived of time as a movement from the past through the fleeting present to the future. We have mistakenly introduced imaginary

boundaries into the territory of eternity and falsely fenced
ourselves in.

We have to understand that time is not something real
that needs to be overcome but an illusion to be seen
through. The ego and time are inseparably linked together
and *each one needs the other to exist* but our real nature is
independent of both. Life outside time has no such boundaries because the past as memory and the future as expectation are *in* it, not around it. The mystic doesn't so much
flee time as embrace all time. He's perfectly free to ponder
the past and future but through the realization that these
ponderings are *present* events, he is never bound by the
past and future. He realizes that eternity is the experience
of timelessness without imaginary boundaries and separa-
tions.

Since the notion of an individual self is only a mental
creation, I understood that there can be no time-self that
exists outside of time and thus *there is no eternal separate
self.* There's only the experience of All-ness, in which
nothing has an isolated existence by itself. If anything
exists at all, it's part of the Whole.

The ego, however, exists only in time but no-time is not
the opposite of time, it's the *absence* of it. Even though the
ego says it wants eternal life, it really doesn't because that
would mean the end of its existence. It's a time-self and
needs the past and future in order to exist.

Since eternity is the absence of time, something that
exists in time can't exist without it and so there's no personal self in eternity. Whatever exists in time can *never*
experience an existence outside of it. In a timeless state,
there are no ambitions, no desires, no yearnings because
these things belong to the ego and if the ego can't exist
outside time, neither can these wants.

There is no separate self that goes into a state of no-time
and since the ego lives in time, it dies in time. *It is not
eternal.* There is no personal you that goes into eternity
because there can't be God's life *and* your life. There is only
one Life and the experience that God's life is the same as
yours is possible *while still on earth.*

Almost from the beginning, I wanted to know how there could be eternal movement and eternal non-movement simultaneously because, like time and eternity, the two seemed irreconcilable to me. Much later I realized that I was thinking in terms of either/or instead of and/both and saw that the distinction between movement and non-movement was just another imaginary division. This boundary only seemed to separate what, in fact, was not separable. It wasn't a matter of movement or no-movement but movement *and* no-movement, both at once.

The two exist as a unity and neither can be separated from the other and this division is just a performance of intellectual gymnastics. Their union, I understood, was the mystery of the Trinity, the eternal non-movement, the Father, with the eternal movement, the Son. The Son is the first movement away from non-movement and the Holy Spirit is the agent of change from one to the other, the transition from non-movement to movement and back again. Non-movement and movement both constitute an indivisible unity and are inseparable forces, Father and Son, each being and becoming the other.

I discovered that there are things that can only be understood upon reaching a certain level of being and one of those things I did not comprehend until later was what Jesus meant when He said that nobody sees the Father except the Son. I always had feelings of spiritual inferiority when I read that because it felt too much like there was some kind of one-upmanship going on. If it was completely outside our field of experience, then why did He even bother mentioning it at all?

Much later I saw the *symbolic significance* of that statement and understood it to mean that the only agency that has direct contact with the Father, eternal non-movement, was the Son, eternal movement. Each is always *becoming the other* and both are personified parts of one movement and I realized that Christ was not a person but the *first cause of motion* away from the Father, eternal stillness. There can never be a time when there was no creation because this first cause always existed and is always creating.

We can never "see" the Father because the only agent that can have union with eternal non-movement is the first cause of motion *away* from it and since Christ, as the Son, is the first principle of movement, this privilege belongs only to Him. The ego plays no part at all in this union and I finally understood what Christ meant when He announced that only the Son sees the Father.

CHAPTER TWENTY-THREE

DIVINE AND PERSONAL LOVE

After the deeper center opened, my first thoughts started to be of God instead of myself. It was as if the divine replaced the role the ego played in my life and now everything centered around It.

I experienced episodes of divine love in the past but the periods were too short and not intense enough to be recognized as such but when these experiences come now, all I want is to sacrifice my whole being to God. I don't want anything left that I can call mine. The feeling is so strong that I would gladly go through any suffering for it and dying for it would be a joy but I discovered that this is God wanting to do this, not me. It's God's life, His love, and God loving God.

The feeling of this love goes much deeper than the personal kind. Personal love always involves an unconscious projection and ends up being the ego loving *itself* in someone else but divine love has a different flavor to it. There's no projection involved because there is no "other" to project anything on, only the direct experience of love itself without a subject or object. The truth of the matter is that there can only be real love when there's no personal self because the ego is incapable of self-*less* love. If it was, it wouldn't be the self. The more we believe in our own separate existence, the less we experience *real* love.

It's as if there is a sphere in my heart area that starts rotating and expanding whenever these experiences occur. One time I was in a parking lot when this happened and the sphere expanded until it was no longer in me but I was *in it* and, at the same time, all boundaries between external objects and myself disappeared. It was like being in the middle of a circle without a circumference and the heart sphere kept expanding until everything, including the sky, was in *it*. Experiencing the absence of boundaries told me that, in reality, *there is no space.*

I saw that I was incapable of manufacturing such powerful feelings and realized that which loved God *was* God Himself. Divine love is an energy whose only concern is to flow outward and doesn't care who or what the recipient is. I used to be afraid of it because I thought heightened sensations like that would hurt but what really scared me was the absence of "me" in the experience. There's no sense of self in it at all.

It's my experience that we go the wrong way if we don't love Truth more than anything else in our lives and that includes loving it more than another human being. I think that everyone who claims to be in love should be made aware that they are projecting their own divinity onto someone else and to see that this feeling is really coming from inside *them*. In a romantic relationship, our inner divinity is projected onto another person and by putting a human being in God's place, we pave the way for serious self-delusion later. It seems unfortunate that western society has us believe that this misplaced projection is the necessary prerequisite for a marriage.

To project our completion onto another is to miss it in ourselves and the only safe relationship for such a projection to happen is a spiritual one between student and teacher, someone capable of holding such a powerful force. When the projection ends, as it always does, the student will be thrown back on himself and forced to stand on his own. Unpleasant as it is when it occurs, this experience provides the indispensable energy for further inner growth.

Everyone misses the mark by falling in love with another person or with their pet, car or bank account. If falling in love with Truth is not first in our lives then our priorities are not in the right order. *Other people should only be used as mirrors to see ourselves and not be carriers of a spiritual projection.* People who want a relationship are really looking for their own divinity but, since reflection is so troublesome and difficult, they prefer to see their inner qualities *outside* themselves. They don't realize that they're making themselves the victims of a ridiculous illusion.

Associated with any kind of love is the topic of sex but no one ever gave me a clear answer as to whether it needs to be given up in order for inner development to occur. It's my belief that complete abstinence of anything is a way *out of life* but we work in life and refraining from overindulgence is what is really needed. With everything, there's a limit to what is necessary and if we restricted ourselves to what is actually required in eating, sleeping, talking, sexual pleasure, etc., this would be abstaining. I'm firmly convinced that *immoderation* is what keeps spiritual seekers in a state of sleep after they have decided to awaken.

I was once shown in a dream that sexual energy is the same force that is used for inner transformation and that this energy, when not expressed *either physically or mentally,* flows back into the person and seeks another outlet. The fact that this energy can be deployed convinced me of the existence of other drives strong enough to change the direction of the sexual instinct and deflect it, at least in part, from its immediate goal. It strikes me as significant that if sexual energy is continually expressed only in its most physical form, it keeps human beings on a correspondingly low level but experience shows that when held in and not acted out, it accumulates a tremendous amount of energy. This activates dormant possibilities in the individual and I've found that, after stimulating a new function, it carries something of its previous character with it. The new activity thus has a sexual *feeling* to it even though it's not a sexual act any longer. That's why the mystical experience is often expressed in erotic terms.

Although it's my personal experience that celibacy aids the transforming process, expressing sexual energy isn't a hindrance to inner development as long as it's used creatively and not misused. Blockages occur only when this force is utilized for other purposes and it's easy to tell when this happens. All we have to do is look for a particular *vehemence and uselessness* of the task performed.

One time I was watching a televised strength competition where men who were just as wide as they were tall competed in pulling trucks loaded with cattle, sawing six foot wide trees, and lifting concrete blocks onto shoulder high platforms. What struck me the most was the utter uselessness of these tasks and I realized that this was an example of sex energy combined with physical energy. The mixture makes for impressive athletic accomplishments but the actions themselves produce nothing *useful.*

Another example is sentimentality and jealousy, which is sex energy combined with emotional energy. The uselessness of these emotions is a key indicator that the sexual drive is being used in the wrong way since sex energy, rightly used, always produces something *creative.* Nothing useful or creative can be achieved when another center uses this energy.

It's my firm belief that emotional extremes, such as sentimentality and jealousy, belong only to the ego since they always involve something happening to a personal self. When this self fades, however, the emotional reactions associated with it also disappear. I discovered that my emotional center had been changed somehow since the opening of the deeper center, not completely shut off but *transformed* so as to exclude radical reactions. There was no flying off the deep end anymore because there was no one there to fly off.

It seems that certain feelings need specific containers in order for them to be experienced and the ego is the container for negative feelings like depression, despair, and defeat. I think part of the reason we experience them is because we're afraid of these feelings and resist them and this is what gives them the energy to continue. It's my experience that they lose their frightening sensation when we just allow them to *be there*.

Without the old nature, the notions of defeat and rejection no longer had any meaning for me and became just words in the dictionary. It seemed to come with the fading of the former self and I saw that immoderate and heavy emotions were only feelings, *not* external facts, and a new kind of fearlessness emerged that wasn't afraid to take on the whole world.

CHAPTER TWENTY-FOUR

THAT THEY MAY BE ONE

A ll inner experiences begin in the unconscious and anything that starts in the depths must eventually surface and "come forth." I saw that spiritual life also begins in the dark just as physical life does and that no internal happening was ever under my conscious control. I was condemned to helpless inactivity and could *do* nothing except watch and let happen.

I'm firmly convinced that we have to wait for a time for understanding to ripen and only when this time is "fulfilled" does illumination come. As with any preparation—baking, roasting, ripening—inner transformation requires a period of respectful waiting and it's useless to wish things could go faster. Spiritual regeneration procreates itself in the darkness of unconsciousness because conception needs stillness and invisibility, not loudness and light, and only afterwards does the conscious mind realize what has happened. The transforming process took place in its own time and in the way it had to. I was merely a passive observer.

My own introspection has shown me that spiritual renewal not only begins in the unconscious, completely unknown to the surface self, but operates mostly according to a lunar schedule. Dreams of unconscious processes usually occurred one month, almost to the day, before

these changes reached consciousness and I seriously
believe that astrological charts reflect the internal, spiritual
growth of the person as well as external events.

I saw that energy for transformation was created mostly
by an internal resistance, a tension of opposites, an "I will"
versus an "I won't" and I think it's important to understand that both these opposing forces already exist within
us. We don't create them and don't need to. We merely
become *aware* of them but my ego didn't want to change. I
saw that the urge to turn over a new leaf and the desire to
remain the same appeared first in hostile form because
they are *complements* to each other. Later I understood that,
since we contain all the opposites already in us, the unconscious standpoint *has* to be the counterpart of the conscious
one, otherwise the psyche would not be complete.

Psychic friction is produced when the conscious attitude
meets an apparently antagonistic viewpoint from the
unconscious and when combined, they create something
new. The conscious and unconscious work synergistically
with each other and are really two activities of a unified
whole, containing within itself all the needed parts for self-
regeneration. Eventually I realized that the conscious and
unconscious are *not* two irreconcilable opposites but a
single process, one always becoming the other. With observation, I found that the unconscious doesn't obey the same
laws as the conscious mind does and that it acted inde-
pendently of any voluntary cooperation on my part. It sent
its messages in dreams, revelations, and inspirations
whether I was ready for them or not. In time, I learned that
it was better to be prepared, accept whatever emerged
from the unconscious, and adjust myself to be in harmony
with it.

There were long, dry periods when nothing internal
seemed to happen and other times when God revealed
what He was doing so forcefully that it was overwhelming.
Many times I tried to influence the spiritually desolate
periods and shorten their duration and found that I could
not. No matter what I did—engage in ascetic disciplines,
pray, inner dialogue, reflect on dreams—I couldn't *make*

any living water flow and apparently that function is beyond our conscious capability. It was like standing on a cliff, seeing all the water below and realizing there wasn't a thing I could do to cause it to rise up and refresh me.

I don't think that a spiritual dry period is necessarily a retrograde step in the sense of a backwards growth but rather represents a necessary phase of development. I used to be concerned when I didn't *feel* spiritual because I thought God had completely given up on me but later realized that feeling spiritual and unspiritual are both part of the journey home. Even if we imagine ourselves to be in a situation that resembles stagnation, we are still developing. Spiritual progression alternates between shadow and sunlight and occurs whether we are consciously aware of it or not.

Dreams of violent underground earthquakes or someone breaking into my house usually occurred just before something new to consciousness was about to emerge from the unconscious. Contrary to what most people believe, not all spiritual revelations are pleasant experiences. We have to remember that the ego consists of walls composed of rigid attitudes that have to be either dissolved, shattered or, in some cases, violently smashed in order for something new to reach it.

One of these shocking experiences was when the inner divinity pushed itself into conscious awareness. About a month before this happened, I heard something suddenly snap inside my head and although it didn't hurt, gave me quite a start, reinforcing my belief that inner transformation reaches down to the cellular level and is just as physical as it is spiritual. Soon after, I had a nightmare about someone who smashed through the wall of my bedroom with a loud crashing sound. In the dream, I got up and walked towards the door, expecting to see a large, burly man but instead saw a little boy standing on the other side of the broken wall. In amazement, I just looked at him because I didn't recognize him. Similarly, unconscious contents not familiar to consciousness can crash through the barrier separating the two and this breakthrough can be a *startling* experience for the ego.

The fact that I wasn't able to influence any of these internal movements or alleviate their alarming character only strengthened my belief that God is in complete control of our internal life and that He's not playing games when it comes to inner transformation. He's dead serious. Since our knowing is not the same as His, we don't have an overview of the whole picture as He does and it took a while before I realized that even His disappearances were part of the plan. Our role is to remain faithful even after His apparent abandonment of us feels final and that, for me at least, was the hardest part of all.

Mystical authors have described the entrance of divine consciousness as a violent break-in and understandably portrayed it in apocalyptic terms. Although the actual moment of realization seems quite sudden and unexpected, such a fundamental upheaval always requires a long period of incubation. It's only when this preparation is complete and the individual made ready that the new insight breaks through in a frenzied eruption.

At this time I understood that the last judgment is not an outer happening but an *internal experience*, the final preparation before the realization of God. It's a period when character aspects useful to the inner kingdom are separated from those that aren't and there was a feeling of apprehension because I sensed that the final judgment, the inner separation, was about to happen in me. I felt compelled to keep looking at a print that I have of Reuben's Last Judgment and realized that all the people, saints and demons in his painting were personifications of qualities in myself.

At the beginning of my search I didn't understand why so much emphasis was placed on learning to be conscious and much later realized that becoming conscious of the unconscious is a necessary step along the way. It's *not* an arbitrarily imposed task. Enlightenment occurs as a result of becoming conscious of our own darkness, *not* by meditating on figures of light, but the difficulty is that most people believe that they're already conscious. They won't try to acquire a function they *think* they presently have. No one makes an effort to dig for gold if he imagines he already possesses it.

Consciousness of our inner nature is an essential ingredient for transformation but we have to *learn* to be conscious and I think this is where everyone misses the mark. It's not a faculty we are automatically born with but an *ability* that has to be acquired by practice, much like learning to play a musical instrument. It's a *new function of the mind* and needs constant exercise in order to develop.

We can't experience the divine without first finding out about ourselves because to do one is to work towards the other but, in my experience, becoming aware of our devilish side is the initial stumbling block. Seeing the unpleasant facts about ourselves is the first step to inner freedom and consists of looking at all the stuff inside that's been either suppressed or ignored. Luckily for us, though, life leads us through the experiences we need for self knowledge.

Learning about our own darkness can be illustrated with a story.

The Fun House

Once upon a time there was a traveling carnival that had a fun house in it. It stopped in every town and advertised that this attraction contained the ultimate challenge. The manager told the crowd that the only rule was that everyone had to walk into the fun house alone and that anyone who could stay in for five minutes would receive a sack of gold.

A businessman volunteered to be the first. He said that facing angry clients gave him nerves of steel and walked into the fun house. Within a minute he came running out, his face covered in fright.

Then a lady stepped up who declared that she had been through five husbands and that there wasn't anything she could not handle. She walked in and a minute later ran out screaming hysterically.

Next a soldier boldly came forward and said that he was trained not to feel fear and walked in. A minute later he came rushing out, trembling in terror.

One by one, the people from the town went in. Those who egotistically boasted that they were the bravest turned out to be the ones who came running out the quickest.

Finally a young boy said he would like to try. The manager opened the door for him and he walked in. Thirty seconds passed. One minute. Two minutes. Three, four, five. He was declared the winner and received a sack of gold.

The manager opened the door to let everyone else see what scared the people so much and there wasn't anything inside except a full length mirror. But this mirror had magic properties. It showed everyone who looked at it what they were *really* like on the inside and reflected everything the people didn't want to face about themselves, all the embarrassing and shameful personal secrets that they kept well hidden. Everyone ran because no one wanted to face the truth about himself.

The fun house represents our personal unconscious. The people who try for the prize represent the ego at different stages and the mirror represents the mind's ability to look at itself, a reflecting ability. Walking in alone signifies that we have to look at ourselves individually, without leaning on someone else. And the sack of gold represents valuable self knowledge that can be gained as a result of courage and perseverance.

In real life, the mirror in the fun house represents the people in the outer world we come in contact with. We need them as mirrors to see ourselves because it's only in relationship with others that we can see what we are really like. Noticing what we project onto others is one of the best ways to do this.

Many people don't continue on the path because it means facing unpleasant facts about themselves. I learned that the ego consists of *imaginary* and false images of how it thinks it is and doesn't want to see the truth about itself because that would mean the end of its domination. It's a fact that anyone who seriously investigates himself becomes a different person because confrontation with the unconscious has a decidedly disintegrating effect upon the self. After starting the journey back home, the ego dissolves and no longer exists *as it was*.

The way to heaven is through what we *assume* is our hell and it takes real courage to face the devil along the way. Not running away from our inner devils is authentic bravery because what we are confronting is *ourselves* but once we do this, the scary furniture in our mental basement turns into valuable qualities. These traits can then be made a part of the surface personality, since it was only our self-righteous ego that considered them unsuitable.

Want to know what your present level of spiritual development is? Ask yourself how much truth you can stand to hear about yourself before you start to get mad. The point where you get irritated shows your level of psychological maturity. A person on a low level gets offended right away, while someone farther along doesn't feel any resentment because he's already exposed himself to himself. You have come a long way if you can tolerate being *called* what you actually are.

Seeing unpleasant facts about yourself means the bursting of imaginary pictures. There is a sense of relief when this happens because you no longer have to pretend to be something you are not. I think it's helpful to remember that if you can take it, *you can make it*.

CHAPTER TWENTY-FIVE

THE SYMBOLIC MEANING
OF THE GOSPELS

One night I had a dream in which I saw a life-sized, and very life-like, statue of Christ on the cross inside a bathroom next to a large altar in a church. The bathroom door was wide open and the sculpture could be seen from the pews and looked very human, not shiny and waxy like religious statues do. I kept looking at it and suddenly saw the right hand move and realized that the figure on the cross was *alive.*

We have to understand that the story of Christ's passion and death is a *symbolic* account of everyone's inner journey. He relives His death and resurrection in us and it's only through Him that we partake at all in this drama. After the deeper center opened, I realized that since my consciousness was still there, something other than myself had died and that all this inner activity was for someone else.

Everyone eventually goes through the same sense of inwardly dying, feels abandoned by God, experiences a period of lifelessness and then spiritual renewal. After going through this process, I understood that the gospels are symbolic stories of *everyone's inner journey* and that the account of Christ is an archetypal pattern of the total

human experience. That's why I'm convinced that the
stages on the way to union with the divine are the *same for
everyone and occur in the same order*. Only the outer circumstances producing these experiences are different.

One issue that has always bothered me was the doctrine
that Christ suffered and died for our sins. There was something suspicious about that because the notion that the
purpose of the incarnation was so that He could atone for
my *future* sins never made any sense. I used to tell myself
that if God knew in advance that I was going to offend
Him then He should have quit while He was ahead. The
question of what His death was all about, however, still
remained unanswered.

The problem, as I see it, is that very few realize that the
gospel narratives are the symbolic story of *every person*.
Christ showed us by His example what we have to go
through for union with God and it's this symbolic feature
that everyone misses. People are so busy looking for the
historical Jesus that Christ's message of *individual transformation* is completely overlooked.

After I understood that what I've been calling "I" wasn't
an entity but an *activity*, namely consciousness, I saw that I
was never changed into anything and that it was God who
transformed Himself in me. It was Christ who experienced
death and rebirth, *not me*. I was like a puppet who mistakenly thought that it was performing its own actions when
all the time it was the Master Puppeteer playing out His
eternal cycle of death and renewal.

All the experiences for this spiritual drama came from
the unconscious, over which I had no control, and I saw
that I didn't cause the death of the self and knew nothing
about the transforming procedure. It's vainglorious conceit
to think that we are the commanders of our inner life since,
if the truth be known, it's only through God that we have
any life at all.

After going through it, I realized that it's not the person
who is transformed into God but rather *God transforming
Himself **through** the person*. It's God that is born and dies in
us in a continual cycle of death and renewal and *this* is the

meaning of the gospels. It was Christ reliving His passion, death and resurrection all over again through me and I had no upper hand in any of the changes that internally occurred. The only thing I could "do" was watch while something else did all the work and that's why I firmly believe that what everyone calls "I" is not an entity but an *activity*, a reflecting action of the mind.

I can't emphasize enough that it's not the person who is transformed into God but God who regenerates Itself *through the person*. Even though we must take an active role as a conscious participant in our further development, it's important to remember that we don't perform any of these internal modifications ourselves because we have no self that *can* do them. Life is a self-reproducing energy system that uses consciousness as a tool to fertilize the unconscious and produce new life.

It was quite a surprise to realize that the birth and death of Christ replays itself in modern man and that the process of divine renewal is just as much alive today as ever. It makes me sad to see how organized religion is unable to recognize the *hidden symbolism* of these narratives and that the priests and clergy who are supposed to be our spiritual guides are just as lost as everyone else. I think it's this pathetic situation of the blind leading the blind that prevents many individuals from experiencing the inner Christ for themselves.

Meister Eckhart in his *Sermons and Treatises* said that Christ as the divine child is always being conceived by a virgin and born in us but never mentioned, as far as I know, *how* this was done. If the inner Christ is always born of a virgin, how do we contact this lady?

During a certain period when I was in the spiritual community, I had recurring dreams of a white bird that left its droppings on me and on a tree outside my window but what surprised me was that I didn't find this repulsive. The confirmation that this was the beginning of wholeness came almost seven years later, when my unconscious "announced" the coming of the inner Christ with repeated dreams containing the symbolism of four, followed by dreams of celebrations. It was then that I realized that the droppings of the white bird, dreamt nearly seven years before, represented the spermatic fertilization of the virgin unconscious and the symbolism of a supernatural conception fell into place.

This made me understand that the virgin mother was the unconscious and considered a virgin precisely because she is not turned towards the outside world and so is not corrupted by it. Fertilized by a spermatic spirit, symbolized by a white bird in our dreams, this virgin conceives the son of a primordial god father and, since this god can only reproduce what he *already is*, the son is always *identical* to the father. Thus God is always begetting a divine son and renewing Itself *through us* and the gospel narratives are symbolic stories of the complete human potential.

It's important to understand that Christ is *not* a historical figure but the name given to a divine creative energy, constantly renewing itself by being conceived in the unconscious, and in this respect our entire human pattern is only a rerun played over and over. The various actors wear different costumes in different time periods but the plot is always the same. It's a closed circle of God reproducing *Himself*.

Seen in this perspective, I realized that the Trinity is not a being but the personification of three different phases of one continuous process of God recreating and then returning to Itself. A lot of misunderstanding about Jesus's sayings is dissolved if we substitute the meaning of Christ *as the divine creative energy* for the words I, Me, and the Son of Man in the gospels. When Jesus talked about Himself, it was this divine energy that He meant and that His Father is a self-contained energy system having within itself everything needed for self-reproduction. So when Jesus said, "*I come from the Father and return to the Father,*" He meant that a divine power, Christ, is always going out from and returning to the primordial creative material.

To experience something is to consume its essence, so when Christ said, "*I have food to eat you do not know of,*" I understood that He meant that only that which is left *after the ego disappears* can partake of the "living bread." The personal self has to first vanish and therefore it can never experience this higher nourishment.

This divine energy was the mystical food that was transformed at the Lord's Supper and the marvel of it is that this mystical bread is alive today. *It's possible to experience it in this life* and is not something unreachable but, at the same time, it is not a personal acquisition. It's an *impersonal Christ-ness* that extends beyond the realm of individual psychology and can never be anyone's personal possession.

It bears repeating that Christ is the mystery that's always renewing itself and this creative power recreates *itself* by experiencing its own "death" over and over. It's a living energy that is continually born in us and in this way, we really are *"other Christs."* Eventually I realized with the deepest humility that I *never* loved God at all and that, the whole time, it was Christ loving God *through me.* The underlying reality of oneness with the Father belongs only to Christ and it was *His* love for God that I felt, not mine.

It was only in retrospect that I saw the whole picture of inner events and what they were leading up to. We don't know the ways of God and often the experiences He hands us aren't understood until much farther down the road. But by comparing my own journals with those of other mystical authors like Meister Eckhart, St. Theresa, and John of the Cross, I discovered that the same inner states are experienced time after time by various individuals and that their writings, like mine, were only stylized attempts to express the inexpressible.

So the gospel narratives are stories about *us*, not an external deity, and reflect our *true human potential*, which is to experience Christ. It amazes me how determined this world is to prevent everyone from seeing that and how deceptively it tries to keep people on the lowest psychological level by telling them to join up and "be all you can be." We will *never* be all we can be if we think that our present, self-centered level is the highest we can go.

CHAPTER TWENTY-SIX

Stages Of The Human Journey

A fter the ego shut off, I was in a better position to have a comprehensive view of the stages it passes through and what follows is a personal viewpoint of the human journey.

It was obvious that, like the experiences in physical life, occurrences for the growth, development and death of the ego had to come in a certain order and since I neither created the self nor shut it off, I realized that something else had to be in control.

Upon reflection, I'm convinced that the spiritual journey goes through two major milestones of selfhood. The first is that of self-centeredness where the person develops and lives through a personal sense of I and the second is the *opposite* of the first. It's the *absence* of a personal sense of I and a more permeable consciousness capable of realizing union with the divine.

This passage through personal selfhood can be divided into three parts. First, the development of a sense of ego or I-ness; second, when the ego looks for gratification from the outside world; and third, when it goes seeking something not of this world and surrenders to something higher.

The first phase of ego development begins in the early years of life, in which the child has no strong sense of I and speaks of itself in the third person. The feeling of subjectivity or I-ness arises when the ego has acquired enough energy of its own and may well be the moment when the child begins to speak of itself in the first person. The ego doesn't yet know the state of inner tension in which an external limitation is also considered an internal one.

Memory at this stage is essentially a disconnected series of ego memories, all centering around the *me* and this sense of me-ness produces the illusion that there is an experiencer having experiences. Exactly who or what this *me* is, though, will not be clear until after it's gone.

The second stage is that of the developed ego, a period in which inner division with oneself arises due to the conscious cultivation of certain personality traits and the suppression of others. This is when the developing ego wants everything for itself and tries whatever this world has to offer—money, popularity, power, possessions, relationships. When one of these fails to satisfy, it attempts the next activity or goes back to the previous one and tries harder.

The essential feature of the developing ego is its *identification* with other people and with everything it sees. Aspects about itself are still unconscious and so are projected onto the outer world and it lives in a *constant state of identification*. Only the person or object it's identified with changes. We might suppose that the person would want to increase his horizon of consciousness but just the opposite happens. He clings to the narrow range of consciousness instead of letting it shatter in the tension of opposites and build a state of wider consciousness.

It's important to understand that it is the nature of the ego to want things for *itself* and that it is incapable of *not* thinking of itself in everything it says and does. It can't love someone or do anything for another because if it does, it does so with the thought of what it can get for *itself* and how *it* could benefit from it. *"What's in it for me?"* is its most frequently asked, but rarely admitted, question.

It's my opinion that most people don't get any further than this stage of development because our society is

designed to keep everyone at the *lowest psychological level.*
Living with a personal self is the *adolescent* stage in the
spiritual life, and a necessary one to pass through, but
neither organized religion nor society provides the environment for going beyond it. Most people never do. Those
who have are seen as misfits and ridiculed if they talk
about life without a personal sense of self.

Being at an immature level, though, is not the real
problem. The obstacle is that everyone at this level *believes
that he's already mentally mature.* The average man never
questions his level of maturity because he mistakenly
thinks that his psychological development automatically
parallels his physical growth. The two have nothing in
common.

Conventional psychology can't come to our rescue
because it hasn't evolved to the point where it considers
the psychology of the *whole person* and can see the ego as
the juvenile phase of the *total human experience.* What's
worse, it reinforces the belief that different physical bodies
mean separate entities in each.

One of the chief characteristics of the self-centered level
is that the person thinks that everyone perceives life in
exactly the same way and that his own perceptions are
completely free of any personal distortion. I've noticed that
people at this level communicate mostly in clichés and talk
a great deal but hardly ever say anything worth listening
to. They think that they are perfectly normal living in their
airtight egotistical enclosures and resist seeing their own
sub-normality. But that's not the major problem. The real
issue is not that people have an ego but that they're *not
outgrowing it.*

I don't think anything endangers our connection with
God more than a successful life in which we forget our
complete dependence on Him and being involved in life
means that the heartaches and disappointments begin to
accumulate. Eventually we come upon an experience so
painful that it makes the ego turn in another direction and
finally admit that the desserts of this world are all sour.

At this third phase of the journey, an important change in the human psyche occurs and previous inclinations and interests begin to change. The essential feature here is a resistance to the inclination of the higher world and a more or less patent desire to cling to the previous, egotistical level of consciousness. It's as if something in us wishes to stay a child, resist the call to spiritual maturity, and remain unconscious of ourselves.

All the ideals that were cherished in the developing ego begin their reversal and we find that we can't live the higher life according to lower values. What we valued as children will be devalued in our maturity. With observation, I found that not only my values tended to change into their opposites but so did my physical body.

The spiritual life is the direction we are meant to go but we have to first find out that the other way was the wrong one. Now the ego hears about Truth and unity consciousness and decides that *this* is what it wants and, with the same vigor that it put into achieving social success and educational accomplishments, it now channels into finding Truth.

I think everyone should know that at a certain point the self doesn't expand and that an inexorable inner process enforces its contraction. This is God calling us home and His way of inviting us to devote serious attention to the inner life. I have observed that people who should have let their egos die long ago but instead insisted on keeping them alive become hypochondriacs, rigid dogmatists, and either applauders of the past or eternal juveniles. I'm convinced that these traits are all pathetic substitutes for the spiritually mature personality but inevitable consequences of resisting God's urge to become whole.

Anyone who insists on living with his old nature remains suspended, stiff and rigid, which is why I think so many people get wooden in middle age. They withdraw from the urge to inwardly develop for fear of what others might think of their inner change and consequently remain fixed like nostalgic pillars of salt. Money making, educational accomplishments, family and social achievement are all egotistical interests and *have to be outgrown*. We can't carry them around with us forever. Whoever tries to do so pays for it with damage to his soul.

Nobody seems to consider the fact that not being able to outgrow the egotistical self is just as pathetic as not being able to outgrow childhood clothes. A forty year old who still wears juvenile clothes is deplorable but exactly corresponds to an adult living with a personal sense of self. A person who fails to trade in his adolescent clothes for spiritually mature ones has made a decision to stand apart from the call to inwardly develop and will mechanically repeat his egotistical lifestyle to the very last.

I firmly believe that the only person who remains vitally alive is the one who continually dies to the past. The beginning of life and its end are utterly different and yet, in my opinion, they have one thing in common—living closer to the unconscious and increased psychic happenings. The purpose of life is to inwardly die in order to realize union with God and the refusal to do this, the way I see it, is identical to not wanting to live. Spiritual waxing and materialistic waning make one curve.

During the third stage, the ego devotes more and more of itself to the spiritual life until it very reluctantly gives its whole life to that pursuit. It does this in a wavering manner over a long period of time until, after having come this far, it figures that it might as well go all the way just to see what happens. At this point, things are looking pretty surefooted for its spiritual life ahead.

But for a long time nothing happens. Doubts enter when the expected inner reward doesn't come right away. Uneasy suspicions creep in. The ego starts wondering if this, too, was just another wild goose chase. *"How long will it take before I achieve union with God?"* is one of its most frequently asked questions.

There is a definite order to the phases of spiritual growth but what the ego doesn't know at this time is that it can *never* be united with God. Before there can be union with Truth, there first has to be the death of the personal self but neither the end of the old nature nor the birth of

divine consciousness happens overnight. Both require long
preparation and respectable waiting times.

In order to be born again, we must first die but in order
to die, we must first awaken. These three possibilities, to
awaken, to die and be born again are usually not set down
in connection with one another and I think this is where
everyone misses the mark. They are different stages of *the
same maturation process* and must proceed in a certain
order, like the cycle of a developing apple tree. First come
the blossoms, then their death and then the growth of fruit.
Similarly, we have to first wake up, then die, and then the
new birth takes place.

But what's needed to awaken us? When we are sound
asleep, an alarm clock is necessary but in deep sleep one
alarm is not enough. A long period of continual alarms is
needed and they must be constantly changed and new
ones invented, otherwise we get used to the alarm clocks
and fall asleep again.

I think that attachment to God is the last stage of the ego
self and submission to something higher is its final heroic
act. Surrender to Truth is the ego's way of saying, *"I'm
ready to die"* and to let a different self take its place. The
disappearance of the ego will come as a matter of course
because submitting to something higher means practicing
anti-ego behavior and undertaking spiritual disciplines.
This is the beginning of its end.

It's important to remember that the dying process of the
ego is *not* a blissful experience but a struggle between
internal forces and each side is determined to win. We
don't have a choice as to whether or not we want to have
this experience because everyone has to eventually pass
through it. We can, however, choose how we *react* to it.

It's an illusion that we can alter the timing of the ego's
death according to our desire. We may as well ask ourselves where we get the impudence to think we can do
something only God can do. We attribute goal and purpose to the development of the ego, so why not to its end?

I think the problem is that nobody sees its death as
actually the *beginning* of a second birth and in both the

greatest living religions, Christianity and Buddhism, the meaning of personal existence lies only in its end. Anyone who cherishes an intellectual opinion on this point has isolated himself from Truth and stands opposed to his own spiritual development.

My dreams showed me that the death of the ego is heralded with rebirth symbols such as changes in locality, river journeys, new dawns and new lands. Even though my dreams announced the ego's dying long before it actually occurred, I was astonished to see how casual the unconscious was of the whole ordeal. It seemed that it was more interested in *how* one dies and whether the attitude of consciousness was adjusted to dying or not.

It bears repeating that it's the nature of the self to be *self-centered*, to want and do things only for *itself* even though it says that it wants and does them for others. One of the greatest shocks for me was seeing that no matter what I did, even if I acted in the name of spirituality, it was the ego trying to glorify itself in some way.

One time I decided to give up spirituality because that way my ego would not be able to use it to promote itself. I had a feeling of satisfaction afterwards and remember thinking to myself, "What a strange reaction to such a serious decision." Later I realized that it was my ego wanting to give up spiritual activities so that it could point to itself and say, "*Look what I'm giving up.*" It's very tricky.

It seemed like a no-win situation because no matter what I or anyone else did, it was still the self doing it but, luckily for us, the ego contains within itself the very mechanism for its own undoing. If this were not so, we would have to live forever inside ourselves and never experience anything on the outside and therefore never experience God. Self-imposed limits have to go if we are to live the free life.

Another time I was talking with a man who could not stop telling me how spiritually advanced he was. He said that he had some inner experiences that convinced him that he was specially chosen for a divine mission on earth. Since it's my experience that the more compelled we feel to talk about something, the more it comes from the ego, I asked him if he was ready to inwardly die to everything he now considered to be himself. He looked at me quizzically for a moment and when he said, *"No,"* I knew that his ego was trying to keep *itself* alive by claiming that it had a special mission. It's very deceptive and will even proclaim itself to be on an assignment from God in order to keep itself from coming to an end.

Since the ego knows it doesn't exist, it fantasizes about being something it's not and delights in thinking that it's a spiritual giant. Most people, when first starting out on the spiritual path, usually imagine themselves to be more advanced than they really are and don't realize their mistake till much later. I know because I was one of them.

Once the ego has been gone through the ordeal of inner dissolution, there's a waiting period in which its energy slowly decreases and the mechanism that kept it going winds down. In my case, this lasted almost two years and the absence of an instantaneous replacement made me wonder just how long this dying process took. During this time, I had no sense of self and no inner life that I knew of, and kept wondering why God didn't send something to fill the inner vacuum or give me any hints of a guaranteed future inner life. I saw that my pleas and demands for an explanation carried no weight and eventually I accepted the internal emptiness and didn't expect anything to come and fill it.

Living with the inner void made me see that there were no supernatural beings I could entice with my prayers and one of the fallacies that came to light at this time was our egotistical presumption that we could influence God at all with our supplications. What we call God is *not* a deity but an intense sensation of life and being at our deepest level and it became evident that He was acting out Its eternal drama of death and resurrection through me. With this in mind, I saw that the divine not only was living through this body but that He also performed all the actions for all the challenges that came along. I no longer did anything for the simple reason that there wasn't any me left *to* do anything. I discovered with the utmost humility that God not only was living through me now but always had. It was just my mistaken belief in a separate existence that prevented that awareness from reaching full bloom and I no longer prayed for anything because I clearly understood that there was no *external deity* to pray to. Life fulfills Itself through human bodies and supplies everything It needs for Its own actualization. I saw that my prayers to God in the past were all for egotistical reasons.

When the inner Christ surfaced, I could only describe this energy as inner freedom and it seemed to be the opposite of a *personal* self. There was still the reflecting action of the mind but now it reflected an inner divinity instead of a personal self and this inner Christ was experienced so strongly sometimes that there was a tendency for me to think that the inner Christ and I were the same. Knowing that what I called *me* was only an activity and not an entity kept me from arrogantly assuming that I was the same as this creative power.

I firmly believe that all selves, ranging from the ego to the inner Christ, are predetermined, predictable, temporary and highly subjective phenomena. It's my experience that a self is not an entity. It's a *reflective activity* at a certain location along the neurological frequency spectrum inherent in the human genetic code. Since the human nervous system is genetically designed to experience only a small band of energy along this frequency range, the point where the neural dials are tuned at any given time determines the "self" that is experienced. If this weren't so, then no one would be able to experience *any* sense of self. Even the Christ self, sometimes called the True Self, is ingrained into the genetic code and that's why I'm convinced that the experiences enroute to this self are the same for everyone and occur in the same order.

I believe that a new sense of self is experienced as each subsequent circuit of the nervous system emerges and that the Christ self, like the others, has a predetermined life span. It is only subjectively real but so transparent that it allows the divine to be perceived much more intensely than the previous selves and is the highest stage we can experience on earth *at this time*, expressed in the gospels by Christ's disintegration into a cloud of vapor as It returned to the Source. I hold that this symbolically depicts that any states beyond the Christ self are not meant for this world.

The way to the True Self goes through the initial period of disappointment and disillusionment by the ego, which then turns towards spirituality, and it experiences the slow dying process. We have to remember, though, that nothing really dies because there's *no entity* there to begin with, only God playing out Its eternal role of death and renewal through us. Before the inner divinity is experienced, I believe that we go through two separate dark nights of the soul, each one lasting anywhere from six to twelve months. St. John of the Cross reported in his autobiography three dark nights, St. Theresa said she experienced two and I also experienced two. From the time the ego energy initially shut off to the time when inner freedom came, there was nearly a two year difference.

Once inner freedom is experienced, though, all the despair is forgotten and the happiness of the divine within is all one sees. All previous heartaches are erased from immediate memory and I discovered that life went on just as before since no one knew about this transformation except God and me. Nothing on the outside changed. I found that what everyone calls God is not a supernatural deity but a *Presence* and that my whole life of praying to God, asking Him for stuff, telling Him what I needed and when I needed it was a monstrous mental deception on my part. Now that It was an inner reality, I discovered that I never really prayed to God at all. It became evident that all my prayers were only directed to my *idea* of God.

In conclusion, the *total human experience* is the passage through two major milestones, the personal self and the divine. Both are part of the human crossing but it must be remembered that neither one lasts forever nor is ours to ally pass away and Christ will experience His death and resurrection all over again. We have to understand that *nothing* belongs to us and that in the end everything belongs to God.

Although the ego has been called a false self, it's my firm belief that there is nothing illusory about it. It's a *temporary* part of the human journey and we have to live through it but we go the wrong way if we use it to pursue anything other than the highest goal. The predetermined route of our pilgrimage leads to divine consciousness and the decision to make this journey is not ours. We can't change its direction, no matter how hard we pray. The only thing we can do is decide whether want to go along with it willingly and enjoy the journey or resist and cause ourselves a lot of pain.

It's as if we are all on a boat and the boat has a prearranged course to its destination. It's pulling us through certain waters, some calm and some rough, and the only thing we can do is choose how we want to pass the time while on board. We can either accept the fact that there is a Real Captain of the ship or insist that we are the little captains of our own separate boats.

How we experience the journey is our choice but no matter which way we choose to react, the passing away of the old self is still a necessary precursor for the egoless life.

CHAPTER TWENTY-SEVEN

THE EGOLESS LIFE

T he ego's question of *"When will I experience union with God?"* has been answered. The irony of the situation is that now there is no personal self to exclaim, *"I have attained this and this perception is **mine**."* The sense of self had to die in order for that to happen and now there is no one there to claim this experience as his own individual possession.

We have to understand that we are never without the urge to look for God but we have a choice as to whether we want to do it consciously or neurotically. To act it out consciously is to work in cooperation with it, otherwise it expresses itself in bizarre compulsions and addictions. The less we realize this spiritual urge, the more it controls us in a negative way.

Modern psychology, which regards the ego as the ultimate realization of man, has misled us because it has not even come close to the true dimension of human potential. Contrary to popular belief, living with a sense of personal self is *not* our highest achievement. Our nature is the same as God's but we can only realize this after the ego has been sufficiently *lived through* and transparent enough to be seen as the nonentity that it is. The less there is of us, the more there is of God and when we disappear completely, only God is left.

Even though we have to play an active role in our inner development, I saw that the process of spiritual death and resurrection was solely God's responsibility, not mine. I didn't know how to produce such sweeping internal changes and it's God who takes this journey for us and does battle all over again with the forces that try to prevent transformation from happening. We don't *do* anything because everything we can call a self vanishes in the process and, if properly understood, self extinction is actually our salvation.

Everyone longs to return home but each of us does it in our own roundabout way, egotistically thinking that we are making this choice or that decision along the way. Every disappointment and heartache is really a nudge from God telling us that we have wandered too far from home but we are so busy believing that we exist as separate entities that it's difficult to see that it's God acting *through us.* He performs all our movements for the simple reason that we have no independent life of our own.

Towards the end of my search, I discovered that I missed the obvious, which was that Reality was right here, right in front of me the whole time and I didn't see it. I used to have a hard time with the notion that spirit is matter but I think it's more truthful to say that matter is "objective" spirit and that this spirit is the *it* everyone is looking for. I egotistically thought that the goal was to come upon something invisible, so this conspicuous "objective" spirit was completely overlooked. I was looking all over for God when He was right there in my living room.

When I was 19, I was shocked to see that nobody was interested in knowing the *why* of it all and now, 30 years later, I'm stunned that people aren't the slightest bit interested in knowing the truth about themselves. They say they are but they are really not. Most want only shallow psychic entertainment and don't want to face their own nothingness in order to experience their own eternity.

People hold on to a sense of self as their consuming preoccupation because they *want* to live in time and be concerned about their "future." If they would stop running and face their own non-existence, they would see the absurdity of their so-called personal concern and 99.9% of all their worries would fall away right there. The problem is that they're terrified of *living without themselves.*

I think that everyone should know that living without himself is not only possible in this life but that it's the *natural* human state in which God intended us to live. Anything else is *un*natural. If anyone comes to you and says, *"I experience eternal life and I can show you the way to God,"* don't believe him. Only Truth can show you the way to Truth and eternal life belongs only to God. No human being can give you something that belongs only to Him.

My personal feeling is that if learning about something couldn't bring about any inner change or didn't give me any insight into myself then it was a waste of time. I saw that knowing the validity of spiritual truths can only be accomplished by *living* them, not just reading or talking about them. With practice they reach down from the mind to become a living reality and known experientially instead of just intellectually.

The mystic is often accused of having wrong interpretations as if it were possible to separate the knowing of something from the experiencing of it. I believe that such a separation is impossible, since the nature of knowing *is* the experience. The journey home is like a spiral movement around Truth and we always come back to where we were, only now a step up from where we began. The whole transformation process is nothing more than everyone's *normal* development and what the ancients regarded as supernatural is only the *ordinary* spiritual maturation required of every human being. Even with this in mind, it still feels like high mysticism when going through it.

Life, as I see it, is one of constant repetition on deeper levels and the whole human journey is alternating periods of sunshine and shade. I discovered that there are unions and mystical marriages at every level and that only by realizing the spiral movement of the interior life can we understand that every viewpoint along the way is valid. Truth itself never changes, only our perspective of it does.

For this reason, anyone who hasn't had any internal experiences finds the statements of mystics unverifiable and hard to accept. Inner knowing is the very heart of mysticism and consists of *experiencing* truths instead of just believing them and thus carries more weight than intellectual spirituality.

In my opinion, the really dangerous people aren't the nonbelievers in the inner life but the swarm of petty thinkers who have already decided that the realization of union with God is only an emotional fantasy. Since conflict is necessary for the creation of any neurosis, resistance to the spiritual life is the *real* starting point for a neurotic disturbance in the individual. One of the functions of the mystic is to help others understand that God can be an *inner reality* and face them in the direction so that they can experience this *for themselves.* It's the inherent possibility of experiencing the new birth that forms the basis of the mystical life and all introspection in general but this requires paying attention to the inner life, persistence and, most of all, devotion to something higher.

However much individuals differ in their conscious minds, they become more alike when regarded from the spiritual standpoint. The mystic sees everyone as twigs broken off from the mother tree, transplanted, and parts that will mature into divine consciousness but this takes personal effort at first. Afterwards, the process gathers momentum and carries us.

I think it's imperative to view the unified state in the context of our overall development and see it as the *normal* state in which God intended us to live. Further development in human beings is entirely spiritual and achieving our full potential means returning to our original unity with God. This should be everyone's first goal in life—to realize that union with God is possible *while still on earth.* God's intervention in the soul's spiritual process of maturation is the grace that accomplishes in a short time what otherwise would take a longer period.

In truth, the unified life is utterly real but if we believe that this state is only as the saints and medieval mystics have described it, we've settled for someone else's account of the journey and blindfolded ourselves to its subjective reality. The writings of medieval mystics in particular have managed to cast doubt on any contemporary experiences, which, by contrast, seem so ordinary and unspectacular. We mustn't let the experiences of other mystics become the gauge of our own because if we do, we will wait for instances of supernatural happenings that may never come at all.

We have been further misled by authors who give the impression that once the soul experiences union with God, it automatically becomes a charismatic being who buoyantly goes forth and sets the world on fire. There is nothing about the unified state that guarantees automatic recognition from others because *nothing on the outside changes*. All that's attained is the ability to live our lives as God originally intended, in oneness and partnership with Him. Any other view is blowing it out of proportion and making the mystical experience into something it was never meant to be.

I found that mystical literature abounds in descriptions of the initial realization of union but by immediately handing out the good news I think these mystics were only generating premature excitement based on the newness of the state. It's all misleading because without distance, they mistook the part for the whole and what we don't hear about is what happened afterwards.

People need to know what it's like *after* the realization of union and I can personally say that life after the experience of Truth is just ordinary living in all its simplicity, humility, humor and depth. It looks normal on the outside but inside it feels *supernormal*. After the initial realization, though, there is a spiritually dry period in which acclimation to the new state occurs and this was symbolized in the gospels by Christ being led by spirit into the dry wilderness. The devil even tried to put doubt into Christ's mind during this period when he started two of his temptations with, *"IF you are the son of God..."* It's a time when doubt enters and the person wonders if the previous experiences were only delusions.

This is the time when the mystic may feel lost and wonder what has happened to all his former experiences. St. Theresa of Avila was so concerned when her visions stopped coming that she started wondering whether she had just imagined them and says so in her autobiography. When the mystical experiences taper off, it's hard not to think that something has gone wrong or that God did not find us worthy enough to keep them coming but from here on, the full extent of the unified life can only be known by actually living it. God will see to it that we have every opportunity to experience the unified life wherever we are and whatever we do. He's not particular about our individual lifestyle.

I'm embarrassed to admit this but now that I've experienced a little bit of Truth, what do I do with it? Do I speak out and risk being misunderstood or say nothing and play it safe?

My dreams told me that I was selfishly keeping it to myself but what good is talking about a mystical experience if nobody else has experienced it? I know that others have all the doubts about this state that I once did and that most believe these experiences happen only to saints and asylum inmates, *not* to ordinary people. Nevertheless, I've decided to speak out.

Having lost a sense of personal self, I have nothing more to lose.

CHAPTER TWENTY-EIGHT

TRUTH IS SPIRIT

Y ou can't bring Truth into your life by praying to It,
by spiritual disciplines, by being good or by ceremonies and rituals. God can't be persuaded by
anything you do because It is spirit.

One of religion's many mistakes is to have people
believe that they can influence God by praying to Him.
Garbled dogmas have misled everyone into believing that
God is a great power that can heal disease, stop wars and
prevent calamities but He cannot give us health, safety or
protection for the simple reason that He is not withholding
anything from us. God does not create any activity without
also providing all the resources necessary to accomplish Its
end because It fulfills Itself through human activity. He
carries the responsibility and does all the work, *not us.*
Thinking that Truth is denying us something is the ego
feeling sorry for itself so it can play the role of a victim and
scream, "Look how much *I'm* suffering." It'll do anything
to convince others of its illusory existence, including
pointing the finger for its self-induced grief at a higher
power that, from its imaginary perspective, is deliberately
depriving it of what it needs. Watch for this in yourself
and don't fall for it when it happens.

I'm firmly convinced that human beings at their present
level of development are still spiritual toddlers. Children

have to be told what to do because they don't know any better and I've noticed that adults unconsciously want to be treated the same way. Human beings have to be *told* what to do and how to behave because they aren't psychologically mature enough to know from themselves. They're very obedient and *want* to do the right thing but most of the time they don't know what that right thing is, so they look around and imitate whatever they see others doing, no matter how stupid that behavior is. Children do this.

When told something by the parents, the youngster always quotes the source of his instructions, announcing that mom said this and dad told him to do that. Spiritual children do the same thing. When I was growing up, it always seemed suspicious to me that the priests were forever quoting an authority figure when explaining higher truths and I believe that our so-called religious leaders do this because they aren't inwardly mature enough to know from *themselves*. But in my experience, this changes when reaching spiritual adulthood because no one can quote authority figures when it comes to inner freedom.

Upon reaching a certain level, there's no longer any seeking for me and mine but rather a release from all personal sense. I firmly believe that the ego has two favorite words, *gimme* and *more,* and frequently uses them in combination with each other but the True Self is just the opposite. Its only desire is to *give* rather than get and I found that the more I gave of myself, the more satisfied it felt. This increased to the point where I didn't consider anything "mine" until I passed it on to someone else, regardless of whether it was something material or a psychological insight.

At a certain stage of the journey we discover that goodness is a quality that belongs to God alone since a nonexistent entity can only possess *imaginary* goodness and, contrary to what religion would have us believe, we don't have to be good to deserve God. It's not that we first become perfect and then He notices us. It's just the *opposite.* We become good only *after* experiencing Its influence because it's impossible to be good on our own. Believe it or not, whether a person is good or bad isn't the determining factor when it comes to experiencing Truth. What really counts is the intensity of our devotion and how badly we want it. We can't bring God into our lives by trying to be virtuous or by rituals and ceremonies because Truth is *spirit* and no one can influence spirit. I think it's a comfort to realize that neither all our sins nor all our stupidities could ever separate us from God because that which created us is also that which maintains and sustains us. When we make contact with this Source, we have reached the Source of all life.

I discovered that outer ceremonies become meaningless when experiencing the Presence within and anyone who thinks they can persuade God by their prayers and ascetic disciplines is only fooling themselves. The problem, as I see it, is that most people don't realize that God is a Presence, *not* a supernatural being, and that He cannot give us anything but Himself. All our nonsensical prayers automatically stop when we realize that spirit cannot be swayed this way or that by our tearful supplications. Remember that no one knows how to influence Truth but Truth knows how to influence us.

It takes time to let go of the belief that rituals and prayer can influence God at all. This Presence is neither an entity that can be invoked nor a supreme being but a Self-maintained and Self-sustaining power. The only right prayer should be either a request to reveal Itself or a meditation of oneness with It. Attempts to personalize Truth or get It to do something for us indicates a lack of understanding of God as spirit, something that cannot be controlled by either you or me. You're growing in spiritual maturity when you realize the futility of telling God what to do and how it should be done.

It bears repeating that any mental concept *about* God is *not* God and has nothing to do with what It is really like. I used to pray to my idea of God when experiencing limitation or when events didn't turn out the way I wanted but I eventually discovered that the real problem wasn't a sense

of lack or unwanted outcomes. It was the feeling of isolation that resulted from thinking that I existed separate
from everyone else. Knowing that we are one with each
other because we are one with God is of no benefit to
anyone until there is a conscious realization of this but as
long as we believe that we are separate and distinct, we
erect a barrier to encountering the divine.

Truth is inner freedom and that's why we can't teach It
to anyone or make It into a religion and I want to highlight
the fact that it's an *experience*, completely independent of
the intellect, and therefore something that can never be
thought about. There's nothing that we can intellectually
know about God that *is* God. It exists on Its own and isn't
even dependent on our having right thoughts about It. In
fact, we could have all wrong concepts concerning Truth,
hate it, deny its existence, ridicule anyone who talks about
it and this Presence would still remain unaffected. God
isn't influenced by our feelings or opinions about Him.

It scared me when my personal concepts about God
started falling away because it felt too much like I was
losing touch with something higher but whatever we can
know about God can *never* be known with the mind. Let go
of any belief that God can change or improve anything in
your life and you will find that you haven't released God
but rather your subjective concepts *about* God, which never
had any possibility of fulfilling your desires anyway.

Believing that we have separate lives is like the branches
of a tree presuming that they are functioning on their own
and exist independent of the tree. We have no branch life,
no personal life that has a distinct beginning or ending but
we *think* we do and that's where the problem lies. Keep in
mind that there is no such thing as the branch life *and* the
Tree life, no such thing as our life *and* God's life. There's
only the eternal life of the whole Tree.

The relationship of oneness isn't really effective until the
moment of contact because until then we remain separate
human beings. Paradoxically, it's only after we **lose** our
personal sense of self, the individual branch life, that we
experience a relationship with the whole Tree. I used to

think that if I cultivated love, I would feel connected to everything but I learned that practicing virtues on the outside produced nothing *real* on the inside. Much later, I realized that the only way to feel unity was to stop believing it's possible to have a branch life apart from the life of the Tree.

Dreams of lightning often occurred before or during periods of sudden eye-openers but what surprised me at these times was that the falseness that was shattered felt *good* to be destroyed. The relief that was experienced at realizing that so much time was spent believing a lie greatly outweighed any unpleasantness of the astonishment. I think it's the nature of inner revelation to be shocking for the simple reason that light only has meaning if it illuminates something dark and enlightenment, therefore, has meaning only if it reveals our inner darkness, showing us how *un*enlightened we were. Remember that the realization of a truth *always* involves the uncovering of a lie and the comprehension of your true nature is directly connected with the exposure of your imaginary existence.

Don't worry about your past mistakes and all the stuff you did that you hope no one finds out about because, even though you were responsible for doing them, they won't be counted against you. Not really. By the time the inner divinity is reached, the self that thought it committed those errors no longer exists and all past sins are completely wiped out. It's as if they were never done in the first place. Whatever wrong you did in the past was done by mechanical forces while you were in a state of unconsciousness, otherwise the transgressions couldn't have been committed. It helps to remember that destructive forces are able to act through human bodies as easily as they do because *unconsciousness is the best conductor of evil.*

Inner revelation is simultaneously both a shock and a consolation but as long as we hold on to any cherished personal belief, no matter how spiritual it seems to us, we will never find Truth. In order to experience what is not us, we have to first let go of everything that we presently *imagine* constitutes us and have the courage to "come out from among them." We have to think in a new way. This entails mentally dropping all notions we have about ourselves and allow Truth to take away our make believe life in order to exchange it for the real thing. Afterwards, the inner divinity reveals itself in direct proportion to the disappearance of the ego and we become authentic individuals on the way home.

CHAPTER TWENTY-NINE

GOING HOME

A fter all these years of searching for Truth, I'm right back where I started. It took all this time for me to see that there was nothing to be achieved, only something to be gotten rid of. There was no one doing the searching, nothing to be attained and what I was looking for was around and within me the whole time. I just didn't see it. I was like a man swimming in the middle of a lake and asking the other swimmers, *"Where's the water?"* The tragedy of this was that they, too, were wondering the same thing.

Finding our way back home can be illustrated with a story.

The Hidden Compass

Once upon a time there was a Lodgekeeper who managed a mountain resort. Many people visited the area to hike and enjoy the natural splendor of the mountain.

One day a guest checked in. After getting settled, he told the Lodgekeeper he was going out hiking. The Lodge-keeper advised him to keep noticing the direction of the sun because there were no trails in the area.

"No trails?" the visitor asked.

The Lodgekeeper explained that as soon as someone made a path, the wind and dust covered it up. *"The sun is your best guide to lead you back to the safety of your cabin,"* he said.

The man assured the Lodgekeeper that he would remember to do this but the thrill and excitement of the mountain overwhelmed him. He completely forgot the Lodgekeeper's advice as soon as he stepped outside.

After walking and wandering most of the day, he decided to head back. Then he remembered that he forgot to watch the sun.

The hiker tried to retrace the way he came but soon lost his sense of direction after the first few feet. He did not see any footprints behind him and then realized that the wind and dust thoroughly wiped out the path he had just made. There was no trail for him to follow back to the cabin.

The visitor panicked and started running but the faster he ran, the more he panicked. The more he panicked, the more he lost his sense of direction. He knew he'd never find his way back before dark without knowing which way to go.

Sitting down on the grass, he put his hands in his pockets and watched the sun get lower.

Soon his fingers encircled a strange object. The traveler pulled it out and saw that he had a compass with him all along.

"I didn't know I had this," he mumbled.

Watching the needle sway back and forth somehow reminded him that he walked south when he left the lodge. When the needle stopped moving, he knew that it pointed him in the direction back to safety.

After the man returned to the cabin, he told the Lodgekeeper about how he got lost and especially about the unexpected compass he found in his pocket.

"I put the compass in your pocket," the Lodgekeeper said.

"You? Why?" asked the visitor.

"Because I knew that in all your excitement you'd forget to watch the sun," he replied. *"And without watching the sun, you'd never find your way back."*

He told the traveler that his compasses are, without question, the most reliable means for making the return journey and that he made sure that all the guests had one on them before they went out.

"Then why didn't you TELL me you put it there?" the man asked.

"Because you'd be offended if you knew I did. I was aware of how you secretly thought you could find your way back without any help," replied the Lodgekeeper, *"but I knew full well you couldn't. Some find their hidden compass sooner than others,"* he continued, *"but everyone eventually discovers that they have one."*

"So everyone always gets back safe?" the visitor asked.

"Everyone," affirmed the Lodgekeeper. *"In the entire time that I've been here,"* he said, *"no one has ever been **permanently** lost."*

⟡

Finding a little bit of Truth within is like discovering a hidden compass in your own pocket. Some find it sooner than others but when you discover it, you no longer need to go around asking other people to please show you their compasses. You have your own.

But *how* do you make contact with this inner guide?

It's there but you have to do some digging in order to find it, like searching for a treasure buried in your own back yard. The treasure exists but you need to know some sensitive secrets about locating it.

The first is that there is nothing for you to create, only something to *get rid of.* You don't have to invent this inner wealth because it's already there. Your job is to remove the obstacles that prevent you from finding it.

What obstacles? Not wanting to change inwardly is one. An unwillingness to forgive others and yourself, a second. And believing that you already have this treasure and there is nothing more to experience, a third.

Another secret is to try and see the inadequacy of your everyday responses to life. Changing your reactions to external events will set new causes in motion and these new causes will inevitably produce new results. *When things change on the **inside**, they produce a corresponding change on the outside.*

Try it. Try going without just one unproductive habit for a week and see what happens.

Let's take complaining as an example. Instead of grumbling when something goes wrong, do just the opposite. *Don't* make a fuss about whatever happened. This will feel strange at first but do it anyway. The issue here is to challenge your everyday habits. When you don't go along with your customary reactions, you're setting into motion powerful forces that will change you internally. This same energy will also attract new conditions and new people into your life who, likewise, will be less complaining. Remember that *the inner determines the outer.* The more *you* change, the more your world changes.

So give yourself permission to experiment with different ways of reacting. Don't shortchange yourself by using the same emotional response over and over again, like getting mad when a situation doesn't turn out the way you expected. Try something new. Keep in mind that each event has its own set of circumstances and that each requires a distinctive reply.

Think it's too late to start?

Never. If you turn on the light in your living room, it doesn't matter how long the room was dark. The important thing is that there was an *internal change.*

A refreshing, new sense of self will start to emerge and it will not be just another rearrangement of your old mental furniture. So don't sell yourself short. Go all the way with discovering your inner compass.

What you have always wanted is already there waiting for you.

CHAPTER THIRTY

What You Can Do

W ant to know which path in life to take? The one
that will make you inwardly grow. *That's* the one
to take.

One time I was talking to a man and describing the
processes of self-observation and projection and urged him
to see as much of himself as he could. He asked if I thought
he might see something in himself that he would not be
able to handle or if anything from the unconscious would
emerge that he could not deal with. I told him that it was
good to see the bad in ourselves and that the only thing that
would be offended by anything from the unconscious was
his phony, self-righteous image of himself.

After talking with him for a while, I discovered that he
had led a sheltered life and went out of his way to avoid
situations in which he would come into contact with new
people. He circumvented predicaments that might force
him to "handle it" and was understandably scared when
faced with the possibility of having to deal with unfamiliar
parts of himself all alone. What we are afraid of on the
inside scares us on the outside and I saw that his desire to
shy away from strangers reflected his fear of facing
unknown "people" in himself.

I told him that whenever we come across unfamiliar
situations either in ourselves or in the outside world that

force us to "handle it," our inner strength grows consider-
ably and eventually we see that we can handle *anything*, no
matter what the outcome. The knowledge that we can face
anything without running away is the key that allows us to
take greater psychological risks. The deeper we go into
ourselves, I told him, the closer we come to God.

If you are not taking any risks and seeing more of yourself then you are not really enjoying life, no matter how
hard you try to convince yourself otherwise. You have to
give yourself permission to feel as confused and as scared
as you want in your spiritual search. You mustn't be afraid
of being afraid because it's only by going *through* your
confusion and fear that you finally come to clarity and
fearlessness.

Upon embarking on the inner journey, it's important not
to take ourselves too seriously. We have to lighten up. We
live in a world where most people take themselves and
their decisions as matters of life and death but I have news
for you. Nothing in life is *that* serious. And don't worry
about making mistakes along the way. For some reason we
feel we always have to make the right decision and forget
that nobody ever found the way home without going
down a lot of dead end streets. We learn through our
mistakes. God will see to it that we attract whatever experiences we need in order to come closer to Him, despite
any wishes that we have to the contrary.

But if *you* are interested in getting closer to Truth, you
need to break away from your present obstacles and put
yourself among others who practice *real* spirituality. Spiritual principles must be *lived*, not just talked about, and
searching for Truth is like being in a spiritual recovery
program. Progress is swift when you're in the company of
like minded people.

Disidentifying with everything you *think* is you plays a
crucial role in this life. Human beings are always in a state
of identification, only the object we identify with changes,
and inner freedom is first of all freedom from identification
and imaginary ideas about ourselves.

One of these illusory notions is that we have free choice and that we are able to turn our lives in any direction we please but we have to see through this false concept. We have to realize that we do not exist the way we *think* we do and that we lose nothing by giving up this notion because, in reality, we have nothing to lose to begin with. The great aim in life is to realize God by first realizing our own *nothingness* and I discovered that one of the stickiest illusions to give up was that of having free choice.

Separating from thoughts and false images is learning a new behavior, a new way of living *without a sense of personal self*. There is an inner emptiness that we will have to learn to adjust to, an emptiness that's both a quietness and conscious awareness of existence, an emptiness that's God Himself. This is our *natural* center.

Imagine someone in prison who wants to escape. He has to familiarize himself with the prison grounds, do the digging and keep an eye out for the guards all by himself.

Now picture five people wanting to escape. They could take turns shoveling, watching for the guards, and if one became lazy or distracted, the others could remind him of his goal. What do you think would happen if ten people decided to make a run for it? Or twenty? They could take turns excavating so that the tunneling would be continuous and make a getaway more quickly. Instead of one person taking a long time to get out, all twenty beat a retreat sooner because of everyone's efforts. That's the value of being in a group of like minded people.

Suppose one of the prisoners managed to escape and now that he knew how to get out, he returned to the prison camp to help the others but to his utter amazement, he finds that nobody is interested in escaping. Upon questioning them, he learns that they do not believe being free is possible and that the only way out is via the midnight express. The ones who do think escape is possible are too afraid to act for fear of attracting attention.

The man discovers that his former cell mates have become so accustomed to jail life that they actually prefer it, believing that their cramped cells are their spacious living rooms. He has a problem because if those in jail think that their cells are palaces, they will never listen to anyone who tries to tell them of real freedom. So suspecting that we are not free *right now* is the first step to inner liberty.

We have to understand that we can escape from our egotistical prisons only with the direction of those who have broken out before us and this, in my opinion, is where most people get stuck. They don't want to admit that they are not already free, so they stay where they are and pretend that their psychological jail cells are comfortable habitats offering shelter from the outside world. They even call the other prisoners their "friends" and unconsciously agree to avoid noticing their neighbors' actual condition in order to dodge the unpleasant task of becoming aware of their own.

But if our neighbors down the block started digging their way out, that would raise the unsettling possibility that we, too, would have to go to work in order to become free. I don't think there is any hatred as bitter as that of a person who is shown his actual psychological condition and told that the purpose of life is not the immediate gratification of the senses. It wasn't for me.

What would you prefer—someone who made your prison life more comfortable or someone who tried to help you see your present, restricted condition so that you could become free of it? Unfortunately, most only want a comfortable prison existence. The hard part is to realize the sobering fact that we are not already free.

People are so used to their imprisonment that they no longer notice it and, what's worse, even take pride in living in their mental slammers. They give themselves catchy nicknames, tattoo psychological identifications on themselves and brag about how bad they are. They're identified with their imaginary existence but, terrible as it is, now they know who they are. Being in an egotistical prison at least provides them with some kind of identity.

I think the mistake most people make is that they believe that there are many individual ways of attaining heaven and at the outermost fringes, that's true. But there is only one way for the personal self to dissolve and that's by self-insight. There will not be any entrance into the kingdom if a person doesn't want to go into his inner basement and see that all the brutality and wickedness out in the world is also *in him*. Once the personal self starts dissolving, which means consenting to inner death, the ways become fewer until there is only one, which is to make all our unconscious parts conscious. This culminates in the experience of a new self.

Find a group or retreat that fosters and encourages *living* higher principles. Life becomes more fun and less of a struggle when you do not have to pioneer on your own and it's the *experience* of Truth that you really want, not just pleasant discussions about it. Read books by others who have found the way. If you're fortunate enough to find someone who has escaped from his own prison, listen to what he says. Just meeting him gives you the reassurance that if at least one other person has found the way back home, *so can you.*

Most of all, trust God at every step of the way. This can *never* be emphasized enough.

ABOUT THE AUTHOR

P atrick Drysdale is an author and lecturer of transpersonal psychology and inner transformation. He received his B.S. from the University of Illinois and his articles and short stories have appeared in metaphysical publications throughout the world, the most notable being *Avatar International* and *Somatics: Journal of the Mind/Body Arts and Sciences.*

Born in Chicago, Illinois to religious parents, his mystical experiences started occurring when he was 19 and although raised Roman Catholic, he left the church at an early age because he was unable to reconcile the religious notion of God as an external deity with his experiences that told him about a divinity within. According to him, *"religion has given us everything but the experience of God, which is what it was originally supposed to do."*

He has dedicated the last 30 years to finding Truth, ten of which were spent in a spiritual community in southern Nevada, *"and I've found something,"* he says. *"Or rather IT found me."*

He openly encourages others to start the journey within and states that the kingdom of heaven is to be found inside the individual, not outside, and at one of his lectures he said, *"You don't have to go to holy mountains or sacred places to find Truth. Even if you've never been inside a church in your life,"* he says, *"it's still possible to experience union with the divine **here and now**. But you have to make the first move."*

A dynamic speaker with enthusiasm that shows, he is able to present spiritual concepts in innovative ways and his books and lectures are sprinkled with encouragement and humor, all the while maintaining the undertone that inner transformation is a very serious business. *"Just because you're serious about being spiritual,"* he once said, *"doesn't mean that you have to go around looking like you just came from a funeral."*

The Journey to No-Self contains a description of his initial mystical experiences, training in a spiritual community, the dark nights of the soul that plunged him into despair and the intense inner struggle he encountered between the divinity wanting to be born and the forces that would oppose it.